EROTIC WARS : WHAT

# DATE DUE

| | | | |
|---|---|---|---|
| | | | |
| | | | |
| | | | |
| | | | |
| | | | |
| | | | |
| | | | |
| | | | |
| | | | |
| | | | |
| | | | |
| | | | |
| | | | |
| | | | |
| | | | |
| | | | |
| | | | |

# EROTIC
# WARS

# EROTIC WARS

## What Happened to the Sexual Revolution?

## Lillian B. Rubin, Ph.D.

*Farrar, Straus & Giroux*

NEW YORK

Library of Congress Cataloging-in-Publication Data
Rubin, Lillian B.
Erotic wars : what happened to the sexual revolution /
Lillian B. Rubin.—1st ed.
p.   cm.
1. Sex customs—United States.   I. Title.
HQ18.U5R82   1990     306.7'0973—dc20     89-25636     CIP

FOR MARCY
*One of the Transition Generation*

# Contents

1. The Changing Scene     3
2. Before the Big "IT"     19
3. The First Time     41
4. Teenage Sex     60
5. The Transition Generation     89
6. Sex, Gender and Power     116
7. The Quest for Relationships     141
8. Sex and the Coupled Life     161
9. Waves, Ripples and Rocks on the Shore     192
   BIBLIOGRAPHY     203

# Acknowledgments

———————•———————

*D*espite the name that appears on the jacket, a book rarely is the product of the author alone. Rather, there are always others who participated along the way. I am fortunate, indeed, to have many such people to whom I am deeply grateful.

First and foremost, I owe a very special thanks to the hundreds of people who so graciously allowed me to enter their private lives. Without them and their willingness to share with me some of their most intimate secrets, there could have been no book. Although I have altered their identities to protect their privacy, I have tried to repay their generosity by telling their stories just as they told them to me, doing justice, I hope, not only to the words they spoke but to the spirit that underlay them.

Kristine Bell served both as a trusted research assistant and as a native informant about adolescent life. She not only made my life easier by taking care of many of the details of the project but sharpened my understanding of the life and concerns of teenagers in our modern world.

My agent, Rhoda Weyr, was, as always, a quiet, steady voice in the background—always available, always thoughtful, always a helpful and intelligent critic.

Roger Straus III, my editor and my friend, was all one could ask of someone who fills two difficult roles in one life. His was the presence that guided the work from its initial conception to its final culmination. His marvelous sense of humor, his warm support, his refusal to join me in those moments when I lost faith in my ability to do the job, substantially eased some of the pain and strain of writing this book.

For several years I have been part of a group of eight—six men, two women—who came together out of shared mutual interests, both intellectual and political. For these years of stimulating monthly discussions and for their thoughtful reading of this manuscript, I want to thank the members of that group: Bob Blauner, Elliott Currie, Troy Duster, David Matza, David Minkus, David Wellman and Norma Wikler.

Kim Chernin, Sam Gerson, Barry Glassner, Dorothy Jones, Harry Levine, Jim Lucas, Nancy Lucas, Walter Meade, Bruce Miroff, Laurie Phillips, Arlene Skolnick and Bernie Zilbergeld all offered helpful criticisms of one version or another of the work in process. Joyce Lipkis—old friend and professor of English—has, in addition, saved me from any embarrassing lapses in the language.

Special thanks go to Kristin Luker, whose careful, critical reading of an early version of the manuscript was extremely helpful in shaping the final product into a better, stronger book than it would have been without her response.

Michael Rogin's wisdom, his unique way of seeing a problem, his unstinting generosity in sharing the extraordinary talents of his mind, have profoundly influenced all my work. This book is no exception.

Of all those who gave of their time and talent, no one was more generous or more important to the final product than Diane Ehrensaft. She not only talked with me about every major idea in this book but read every word of every draft, bringing her sharp, critical mind to bear on each problem that needed resolution. For that, and for the years of friendship that have given me so much pleasure, I am deeply grateful.

For over two decades Barbara Artson has always been available to lend her support to the work I was doing, to talk with me about the problems I was encountering, to engage with me in a stimulating and provocative exchange of ideas, and to read and comment on every word I wrote. To her, my fictive sister and dearest friend, my heartfelt thanks for a relationship that has enriched both my intellectual and my personal life.

As a member of what I have called here the "transition generation"—the people who made both the sexual and the gender revolutions—my daughter, Marcy Rubin, was part inspiration, part a splendid source of information and understanding as I struggled to make sense of the data I had gathered. For this, and for the many rich rewards and pleasures our relationship has brought to my life, I dedicate this book to her.

Finally, there is my husband, Hank Rubin—friend and lover,

supporter and critic, companion in all the many areas of living. How does one say thank you to one who fills so many corners of a life, whose love and constancy have been the foundation on which both my personal and my professional life have been built? Sharing life with a writer means putting up with long periods of withdrawal and preoccupation, and/or listening endlessly to ideas as they emerge and develop. Never once has he complained; never once has he let me know in word, deed or gesture that he wished it were otherwise. For this, and for all the daily ways in which he makes my life better, happier and more comfortable, there are no words to express adequately either my gratitude or my love.

LILLIAN B. RUBIN

*New York City*
*December 1989*

# EROTIC
# WARS

# 1

## *The Changing Scene*

$S$ex! Say the word and instantly our mind leaps into action. Like scenes from a film, images flash by, remembrances of real experiences, fantasies of those we wish we'd had. Memories of pleasure, excitement and joy live side by side with the moments of anxiety, disappointment and shame. We recall roads not taken, opportunities missed, uncertain about whether to feel regret or relief. And along with it all there's a yearning, a longing for something that seems to elude us, something we missed perhaps, some pleasure not experienced, some promise not fulfilled—something . . . something . . . something that has no name.

"What a subject!" friends exclaimed when they heard I was flying all over the country talking to people about the sexual revolution, asking about the intimate details of their sex lives, probing not just their sexual experiences but their feelings about them. "It's great," they said. "But what made you start working on it?"

The easy answer is that, during the waning years of the 1980s, my attention was caught by the contradiction between my own observations of the sexual behavior and attitudes of the people around me and the media pronouncements that the AIDS crisis had sounded the death knell for the sexual revolution. Every time I'd read another newspaper or magazine story about how we were in the midst of a return to the sexual conservatism of the past, I'd wonder what these writers and reporters knew that I didn't. What did they mean when they said the sexual revolution was over? Who were they talking to? Surely not the women and men I'd met in over two decades of doing research and writing on intimate relationships. Certainly not my straight single friends and colleagues all around the country, nor the patients who filled my clinical practice, nor the teenagers who were becoming sexually active at younger and younger ages.

It's true that the conservative electoral victory of 1980, which ushered in the Reagan years, gave impetus to the growth of a highly politicized, repressive response to the enormous social-sexual changes of the decades of the sixties and seventies. The liberation of female sexuality, which has been the most significant consequence of the sexual revolution, and the struggle for greater equality, which has been the charge of the gender revolution, have brought an increasingly vocal counterattack from conservative leaders, legislators and courts across the land. Despite all the noise, however, it seemed to me that we knew little about what effect these campaigns to turn back the clock were having on the private lives of the people to whom they were addressed.

But there's another answer to the question about what started me on the path to this study, one that reaches back into my own life. I was first married during World War II, a virgin, a girl who followed the rules of her day, who would never have thought to "go all the way." It wasn't I alone who drew the boundary. My husband-to-be was an active participant in protecting my honor, his sense of sexual "rights and wrongs" well matched with my own.

Then, on the day we were married, it all changed. Just because a few words had been spoken, a benediction given, I was expected to drop the restraints that had circumscribed both my sexuality and my sexual activities until then. It wasn't fun. Not for me, not for him. My body said, "Let go"; my mind wouldn't let me. "What would he think if I did?" I asked myself. But it wasn't really a question; I knew the answer. Nice girls don't!

How do we learn these sexual rules? I don't remember anyone explicitly saying those words to me. Yet I knew, as surely as I knew the time of day or the day of the week. For the sexual norms of an age are passed on to the young in a thousand unseen and unspoken ways, as much in what is *never* said or named as in what is.

I swore to myself that no daughter of mine would ever suffer the struggle with sexual repression that had been mine. I would bring her up to feel differently about her body, her sexuality. Little did I know how much help a rapidly changing sexual culture would provide in that task. Nor what conflicts those changes would stir inside me as I watched my daughter enter a life so different from my own. For in the brief span of one generation—from the 1940s to the 1960s—we went from mothers who believed their virginity was their most prized possession to daughters for whom it was a burden.

Intellectually, I knew the young women of my daughter's generation were right to cast off the old sexual norms, to insist upon their right to express their sexuality openly, freely and fully. My own life experience had taught me something of the cost of those repressive norms with which women had lived for so long. So in my head, I applauded their efforts. Emotionally, however, it was another matter. My heart cried out, "This is my child, my flesh. She could get hurt, exploited, damaged." Damaged! A word from my past, when a girl who "slipped" was considered "damaged goods." For my daughter, an alien notion. I could imagine her saying to me, "Damaged? What are you talking about, Mom? How could I be damaged?"

I struggled silently with myself, watching, wondering, worrying, not just about my own daughter, but about all the other mothers' daughters who were caught up in the sexual revolution.

"What, if anything, should I be saying to my daughter?" I asked myself. For a long time I had no idea. By the late 1960s when these questions were upon me, her life, the world she was living in, were very different from the one I had known. What use could my experience possibly be to her? Yet there was a certain virtue in the distance my age and my own life circumstance gave me. While not *in* the sexual revolution, I was *of* it, touched by the depth and breadth of the changes that were going on around me, exhilarated by the permission they afforded for the release from yet another level of sexual repression. At the same time, I could see the possibility for problems ahead. "Sexual freedom," I finally said to her one summer day as we walked across the lovely, hilly terrain of Berkeley's Tilden Park, "is about choice. It's the freedom to say no as well as yes."

Was it on that day more than twenty years ago that my work on sexuality began? Or the day before, when I was still haunted by what words of wisdom I might have for my child? Or the one before that, when I listened to the brave words being spoken, watched the bold deeds being done, by the young women of my daughter's generation, and wondered: Were we, as a society, ready to accept the sexual freedom they were insisting upon? Were they?

Two decades later, it was time to answer some of the questions that troubled me then. I started the research for this book with a series of questions: What happened to the sexual revolution? How do the women and men who made it feel about their past? Their present? How have succeeding generations internalized and institutionalized the changes for which their older sisters and brothers fought? What changes in sexual attitudes and behavior have taken place over the years? How well do behavior, attitude and feeling match in this difficult and delicate arena of human life?

If we're to understand the sexual revolution, however, it cannot be studied in isolation from the other movements of its time, in particular two others with which it has been intimately entwined: the gender revolution and the psychological revolution. Therefore, I asked also: How has the gender revolution, with its demand for reordering traditional roles and relationships, affected male-female sexual interactions and behavior? What effect has the increasing psychologization of everyday life—what I call the therapeutic revolution—had on sexual expectations, attitudes and behavior? How have the sexual revolution and its companions, the gender and therapeutic revolutions, influenced our lives and relationships, in bed and out?

As in all my previous work, I was interested not just in what people *do* but in how they *feel* about what they do. For to dwell on an act without understanding the feeling behind it is to miss a profoundly important dimension in human experience—the *meaning* people attribute to their behavior.

Since the only way to understand those deeper levels of meaning is to talk to people directly, my search for the answers to the questions that were puzzling me took me into the lives of 375 people—75 teenagers, ages 13–17, and 300 adults, ages 18–48—each of whom submitted to a very long, in-depth interview about the intimate details of their sexual history and its meaning to them. In addition, there were 600 others, mostly college students, who returned the thirteen-page questionnaire I distributed in eight colleges and universities around the country. This book, therefore, is a distillation of the sexual histories and experiences of almost a thousand people, heterosexuals all, who live in cities throughout the country, come from diverse class and ethnic backgrounds, are engaged in a wide variety of occupations from factory workers to investment bankers and most jobs in between, and represent a wide range of beliefs from Christian fundamentalism to agnosticism and atheism.[1]

The research was directed at heterosexuals only, not because I think the experience of homosexual men and lesbians is unimportant or irrelevant to the state of sexuality in our nation today. Far from it. No one who has lived through these last decades can deny that there are important ways in which the gay and lesbian movements have affected both our behavior and our thinking about sex and sexuality. Still, as I planned this work, it became clear to me that the issues of one or the other present more than enough complications for a single book.

In all my earlier work, I have always had a neatly organized theoretical perspective to map the way as I wrote. But this time that comfort was not to be mine. For the data I have amassed do not lend themselves to easy answers, nor do they fit neatly into any existing theories about heterosexual sexuality in America today.

I start with one basic proposition, however: Whatever else we may say about sex, it is at least as much a social and psychological phenomenon as it is a biological one. Even the gender differences in sexuality are profoundly influenced by the commandments and constraints of the culture. Certainly estrogen and testosterone make some difference in how men and women experience sexual need and desire. But the larger differences between us reside in our heads, not in our hormones, not even in our genitals. Thus, whether we accept the sexual restrictions of our age, struggle against them, or vacillate somewhere between the two, the context is defined by the historical moment through which we are passing. How else explain the various shifts and changes in sexual norms that have taken place over the life of our nation?[2] How else explain the enormous changes of these last twenty-five years?[3]

The story I have to tell is one of sex, gender and power and of how these have interacted with each other from the beginning of the sexual revolution until the present. It is the story of heterosexual sex among adolescents and adults—of what they do and why they do it, of how they feel about their sexual interactions and what they would change if they could. It tells of the differences in how women and men experience their sexuality and of their efforts to bridge the gap between them. And it is a narrative of the new dimensions in sexual relationships and of the new levels of pleasure and satisfaction which, paradoxically, have been accompanied by a set of heightened expectations that reveals yet another layer of complaint and dissatisfaction. Above all, it is a tale of change of almost staggering proportions in relations between men and women, not just in response to the sexual revolution, but also to the gender revolution, which followed so closely on its heels. And, at the same time, it is also a story of extraordinary stability, of women and men in the eternal search for meaning and for relationships, and of the power struggles that continue to engage them.

In the public arena, sex screams at us at every turn—from our television and movie screens, from the billboards on our roadways, from the pages of our magazines, from the advertisements for goods, whether they seek to sell automobiles, soap or undergarments. Bookstore shelves bulge with volumes about sex, all of them dedicated to telling us what to do and how to do it. TV talk shows feature solemn discussions of pornography, impotence, premarital sex, marital sex, extramarital sex, group sex, swinging, sadomasochism, and as many of the other variations of sexual behavior their producers can think of, whether the ordinary or the bizarre. Even the comic strips offer graphic presentations of every aspect of adult sexuality.[4]

But in our private lives it's another matter. There, sex still is relegated to a shadow existence, and silence is the rule. There, the old taboos still hold: sex is a private affair, something we don't talk about, not with friends, often not even with lovers or mates. How many of us know anything about the sex lives of friends or relatives? What do we know about the sexual relationships of even our nearest and dearest? What turns them on; what leaves them cold? "It's amazing, my sister and I are very close and, can you believe it, I don't even know if she has orgasms," remarked one sexually sophisticated and experienced woman. It's this peculiar combination of public discourse and private silence, the paradox of a "society that speaks verbosely of its own silence," as Michel Foucault has put it so crisply,[5] that is one of the hallmarks of sex in our age.

Throughout our history the official sexual ideology has lived side by side with a deviant sexual reality. Most of the time, such deviance from "respectable" norms is silent, people doing what they want quietly and privately. Because the behavior is shrouded in secrecy, it is invisible in the public domain and, therefore, no threat to the established codes of sexual conduct.

But every now and then, a group of sexual radicals appears, women and men who often are part of the intellectual community of thinkers and writers. Unlike the quiet ones, their aim is not to make some surface adaptation to social values so that they can do what they please without interference. Rather, they self-consciously set themselves apart from respectable society and confront it with its hypocrisies, contradictions and failures.

Since their purpose is to force upon society a new and broader set of sexual options, they seek public notice rather than hide from it. Public censure and punishment may be theirs, but it's a price they're willing to pay to get their message heard. The more their sins are denounced from pulpits across the land, the closer they come to achieving their goal. For in sexual matters as in all others, as public consciousness of alternatives grows, behaviors that once seemed aberrant, even bizarre or disgusting, become possible for some larger segment of the community.

The bohemians of Greenwich Village in the early part of this century were such a group—young women and men determined not just to live lives that were sexually free, but to do so proudly and openly. The hard shell of sexual repression that marked the Victorian era was already showing cracks when the bohemians came on the scene. But they were the first to make sex a political issue, part of a larger agenda of radical social, cultural and political reform.[6] In calling attention to their unorthodox sexual behavior, they were also the first to purposefully make it a visible public statement.

Their daring lifestyle, their insistence that women were sexual beings, that marriage and sex need not necessarily go together, dazzled the media and gave them the public notice they sought. As word spread, their message captured the imagination of the middle-class college youth of the era, who soon took up the banner, and the sexual revolution of the twenties—a revolution in manners and mores as spectacular and profound as any we have yet seen—was on in earnest.

The strict parental supervision that had until then marked the social life of the unmarried young was out. Roadhouses and dance halls with no chaperones in sight replaced the carefully supervised meetings of the past. Alcohol, made illegal by Prohibition, was consumed with abandon. Dance styles went from cool to hot as the Charleston and fox-trot replaced the waltz. The syncopated rhythms of jazz bands heralded the birth of modern popular music. And while premarital sexual intercourse still was unacceptable, women's sexuality came out of the closet. Petting parties that included "everything but" became common events in campus social life.

Just as the bohemians had before them, the behavior of the campus crowd scandalized the keepers of the public morality. But these were not some disreputable creatures with foreign ideas; these were the children of the stable, law-abiding, decorous middle class, the very foundation of respectable society. Pulpits shook as preachers roared; campus administrators and professors agonized; and the media had a field day. Through it all, the students danced, drank and found quiet corners in which to explore each other's bodies.

Before long the very behaviors that were creating such an uproar were adopted by many of the same adults who earlier had condemned them. "By 1923," wrote F. Scott Fitzgerald, "their elders, tired of watching the carnival with ill-concealed envy, had discovered that young liquor will take the place of young blood, and with a whoop the orgy began."[7]

No longer would women suffer the tight corsets, the clothes made of sturdy fabrics that covered their bodies from neck to ankle. Not for them the long hair restrained in a prim bun. Corsets were abandoned; hair was bobbed and seductively waved; body contours were visible under the light, filmy fabrics that clothed them; silk stockings covered legs that were on display as skirts rose to uncover a knee.

Closer to our own time, there were the Beats of the fifties. Militant in their disillusion, flaunting their disrespect for the social codes of the day—whether in style of dress, work ethic or sexual behavior—these hostile, alienated youth outraged respectable society for a decade. But we were not far into the sixties when it became clear that what the Beats of the fifties had started, the disaffected college youth of the sixties would finish.

These were the young people raised in the fifties, the post-World War II decade that celebrated traditional role divisions and gender differences; that extolled togetherness with the slogan "The family that prays together stays together"; that equated cleanliness with godliness, godliness with capitalism, propriety with success. Unlike the youth of the twenties, whose rebellion was almost entirely in the service of cultural and sexual change, the students of the sixties sought to change both politics and culture, calling into question the whole structure of the society they were raised to revere. They joined the sit-ins and demonstrations of the Civil Rights Movement, turned college campuses upside down with their protests against the Vietnam War, started the Women's Liberation Movement to challenge not only the prejudice and discrimination against women, but the whole structure of relations between the sexes. At the same time, they fought the administration of their colleges and universities on everything from the curriculum to the parietal rules that had for so long governed dormitory life.

Parents sent their well-groomed, clean-cut children to college, their suitcases stuffed with the "right" clothes, and watched with dismay as their daughters came home in miniskirts so short that they barely covered their bottoms, and their sons in scruffy jeans, long hair and beards. Or worse yet, sporting the beads, bangles, robes and other exotica of the hippie era. Words like "acid" and "grass" became part of the American vernacular as drugs replaced alcohol as the high of choice. And the music of the Beatles, which had shaken the nation a few years earlier, suddenly seemed sedate.

Although women's sexuality had been widely and openly acknowledged since the twenties, until the sixties its socially accepted expression was confined to the marriage bed. At midcentury, therefore, it still took an elaborate seduction scenario to get a "good" girl into bed, a script that operated on the assumption that she didn't *really* want to, but could be swept away by forces outside her control.

Then came the sixties and the sexual revolution. The restraints against sexual intercourse for unmarried women gave way as the Pill finally freed them from the fear of unwanted pregnancy. Seduction became abbreviated and compressed, oftentimes by-passed altogether, as women, reveling in their newfound liberation, sought the sexual freedom that had for so long been "for men only." The assumption of the era was that she wanted sex as much as he did, the only question being whether they wanted to do it with each other. Young people lived together openly, parading their sexuality before their parents' outraged and bewildered gaze.

By the end of the decade, the sexual revolution had heated up and spread out well beyond the campus gates. The impersonal, casual sex that flourished in the singles bars during the decade of the seventies became the emblem of the age. Sexual intercourse among single adults had won the day.

Since then the Gay Liberation Movement has brought homosexuality out into the open and forced it into the consciousness of the straight world; feminists have significantly changed the face of relations between men and women; and the words "sexually active teenagers" no longer sound like a contradiction in terms. Changes so dramatic that they moved a bright, thoughtful, tousle-haired 15-year-old boy I met to muse, "I guess sex was originally to produce another body; then I guess it was for love; nowadays it's just for feeling good."

By the 1980s, first herpes, then AIDS became household words, while a host of other sexually transmitted diseases, many of them so rare they were generally unknown until then, became epidemic, part of the reality of everyday life.[8] As these diseases increasingly brought illness, infertility and death, newspapers, magazines and television began to feature stories proclaiming the death of the sexual revolution and the return of the sexual conservatism of the past.

On the surface, it seems a reasonable reading of the public

response. Men, women, even teenagers, speak of their fears. A nationally syndicated feminist columnist writes about how adult daughters are so frightened of disease that they listen with wistful yearning to their mothers' horror stories of the bad old days when sexual freedom was only a dream, when women couldn't get birth control, when honorable maidens were expected to marry before they could experience the joys of sex.[9]

But we don't have to look far below the surface to see a picture that's much more complicated than the spoken words suggest. When we do, we see a wide gap between attitude and behavior, between what people *say* they're frightened of and what they *do* about their fear. We see women and men, young and old, *speak* their fears about AIDS but *act* as if they had nothing to be afraid of.[10] We see also the same daughters who seem to long for a safer age engaging with ease and aplomb in sexual behaviors their mothers didn't dare dream of, and defending their right to do so without question or criticism. "I was about 16 and I had this friend—not a boyfriend, a boy *friend*—and I didn't know what to give him for his birthday, so I gave him a blow job. I wanted to know what it was like; it was just for kicks," explained 20-year-old Ellen, a student at the University of Michigan, without a trace of embarrassment or self-consciousness.

There are changes in process, to be sure. Condoms have displaced bubble gum in displays at drugstore cash registers. Business at singles bars in cities like New York, Los Angeles, Atlanta and San Francisco is far less brisk than it was ten years ago. Both women and men are more likely than they were a decade ago to choose their partners with at least some modicum of care. But notice the words "modicum of care," for they are deliberately chosen.

Perhaps it's true that there generally is a decrease in the *number* of sexual partners any given person will take.[11] And it may also be true that larger numbers of women and men than in the seventies don't fall into bed on first meeting. But this says nothing about what happens on second and third meetings, often with very little more information than people used to have on the first one. More important, how people choose their partners tells us nothing at all about the *content* of sexual behavior or about the *meaning* people attribute to it. Surely this is at least as significant in assessing the life or death of the sexual revolution as the number of partners people take.

After speaking with hundreds of people across the country, it seems clear to me that while the contours of the sexual revolution may have changed, this in no way signals a return to the past. We need only look at the difference in the sexual histories of the 40-year-olds and the 20-year-olds to see how deeply the transformation in sexual norms we have witnessed has been integrated into the culture, consolidated into sexual behavior and internalized by the majority of adults, as well as teenagers, in the country. Indeed, as the pages that follow will show, the changes wrought by the sexual revolution of the sixties and the decades that followed have profoundly altered both the sociology and the psychology of sex in the United States, not just for the generation who made the revolution and those who came after, but for those who preceded it as well.

## A Note About Studying Sex

Always before, I have gone into a research project confident that my many years of experience as a psychotherapist would enable me to get people to talk openly about all kinds of highly personal issues in their lives. But this time, I entered the field with trepidation. Would people be willing to talk with me about something so private as sex? This, after all, is *the* forbidden subject, the one we don't touch even when we're open to discussing all other aspects of private life.

I spent weeks thinking about it, planning strategies, trying out different approaches in my head. I was surprised, therefore, at the alacrity with which so many women and men, strangers all, accepted my invitation to participate in the research for this book. As I met and talked with them, however, several things soon became clear. First, in this era when so much has changed, when sex is both so public and so private, people feel a need to talk about it, not in some impersonal, abstract discussion of what "people" do, but about their own sexual behavior, attitudes, feelings and fantasies. The interview allowed them to process their experiences in some systematic way, to articulate their feelings about them, to make order out of them so that they attained some coherence in their inner life, and, most important, to assign meaning to those experiences so that they could make sense out of them.

Second, they wanted to share their sexual experience with someone they could define as an expert; to check it out, to ask, as so many did, if they were "normal." Who better to meet this need than a total stranger, one who is perfectly safe precisely because she's part of a fleeting encounter, never to be seen again? Indeed, the relative anonymity the research interview permits makes it a safer milieu than most for the discussion of this tabooed subject.

Not infrequently, in fact, the men and women I met in the course of the research for this book said that they had never talked so freely about sex to their therapist. For even in the consulting rooms of psychotherapists of all persuasions, sex is, at best, a topic that makes both therapist and patient uneasy. The intensity of feelings the therapeutic relationship engenders, the mutual fantasies of seduction that are so common, the transference and countertransference issues that arise—all these spell potential danger, making it easy for therapists to collude with their patients in silencing discussion about sex there. It doesn't take much; no words are necessary. The slight hesitation when the subject arises, the shift of the body in the chair, the loss of eye contact, the failure of words—any one is enough to send a message to the patient that *this* subject is too hot to handle.

Finally, the willingness of the people I interviewed to speak so openly about the most intimate aspects of their sexual feelings, fantasies, attitudes and behavior is, in itself, evidence of the depth and breadth of the sexual revolution. I don't mean to suggest that people didn't have moments of discomfort as they struggled to describe their sexual fantasies or just what they do when they masturbate. But they were a model of ease when compared with the way people responded two decades ago, when I asked questions that seem tame by today's standards. Indeed, since it was so difficult then for people to talk about the more mundane aspects of their sex lives, I didn't dare ask many of the questions I pursued in this research.

Now, in pursuit of understanding the changes that have taken place, how they have been consolidated and internalized, and what meaning they have in the lives of the people who must live them out, we turn first to their early sexual experiences, to the time before the veil of mystery has fallen, the time before, as teenagers still say, the big "IT."

---

1. About 5 percent of the sample are black, another 5 percent Asian and 2 percent Latino. The class distribution is roughly 30 percent working class, 45 percent middle class and 25 percent upper-middle-class professionals, each group divided approximately equally between men and women. There are roughly four different generations represented. Those 35 and over, whom I take to be the revolutionary generation—the women and men who were responsible for the assault on the then existing sexual norms. The 25–34-year-olds, who came of age during the sexual revolution and were the first inheritors of the new freedoms. The next two—the 18–24-year-olds and the 13–17-year-olds—are separated conceptually by less than a decade because the passage from high school into the world of work or college has, for a long time, been an important sexual divide.

2. For an excellent historical analysis, see John D'Emilio and Estelle B. Freedman, *Intimate Matters: A History of Sexuality in America* (New York: Harper & Row, 1988).

3. The heterogeneity of our society makes it impossible to make any statement about sexuality that applies to all groups at any given time. Class, ethnicity and race all make a difference in the *particular* rules that regulate sexual attitudes and activity. Nevertheless, each historical period is marked by an ethos that dominates the sexual scene and defines the parameters of acceptable sexual behavior for most of its citizens. So it is with the one we are now living in, just as it has been for the decades since the sexual revolution came upon the American scene in the early 1960s.

4. For an interesting survey of sex in the comic strips, see Maurice Horn, *Sex in the Comics* (New York: Chelsea House, 1985).

5. Michel Foucault, *The History of Sexuality* (New York: Vintage Books, 1980).

6. For a detailed analysis, see Ellen Kay Trimberger, "Feminism, Men, and Modern Love: Greenwich Village, 1900–1925," in Ann Snitow, Christine Stansell and Sharon Thompson, eds., *Powers of Desire: The Politics of Sexuality* (New York: Monthly Review Press, 1983).

7. "Echoes of the Jazz Age," in *The Crack-Up* (New York: New Directions Publishing, 1945).

8. The Centers for Disease Control in Atlanta warn that we can expect over 4 million new cases of chlamydia each year, 1.8 million cases of gonorrhea, 1 million cases of cytomegalovirus, 1 million cases of genital warts, a half million cases of genital herpes, to name just a few. Some of these—genital herpes, cytomegalovirus and, of course, AIDS—are presently without remedy. Others can be cured with no lasting ill effects *if* treated early enough. Unfortunately, diagnosing them in time to ensure successful treatment is uncertain at best, since several of these diseases show no symptoms in the early stages. Excluding AIDS, this panoply of sexually transmitted diseases now accounts for more than 13 million cases and 7,000 deaths annually, according to the U.S. Public Health Service. Among the men and women represented in this study, over one-third have suffered at least one of these diseases, many more than one.

9. Ellen Goodman, San Francisco *Chronicle*, February 10, 1989.

10. A study sponsored by the Alan Guttmacher Institute surveyed women 18–44 who were at risk for pregnancy or disease (i.e., women who were sexually active, fertile and not pregnant or trying to get pregnant) during the years 1982–1987. Their findings show that the increase in condom use was negligible—from 12 percent to 16 percent—during this period at the height of the AIDS scare. Jacqueline D. Forrest and Richard D. Fordyce, "U.S. Women's Contraceptive Attitudes and Practice: How Have They Changed in the 1980s?" *Family Planning Perspectives* 20, 3 (May–June 1988): 112–118.

11. There are no good data on this issue, but there are some structural reasons to suspect that the reverse is actually true. As people live outside marriage for longer and longer periods, they are likely to have more, not fewer, partners over the course of a lifetime.

# 2

———◆———

# *Before the Big "IT"*

*F*or generations, the words "everything but" have told the story of teenage sexuality. The awkward early gropings become more daring with time; the boy's hand moves from breast to vagina; the girl's tentatively touches his penis, then withdraws in surprise.

"I didn't know it would feel like that, so hard. I guess it scared me that first time, maybe for a while afterwards, too. I really didn't like touching that thing," recalled Marsha, a 32-year-old hairdresser from Chicago, with a grimace.

"Why did you do it, then?" I asked.

"I don't know," she replied with a shrug. "I guess because I was curious; you know, the other girls were giggling and talking about it. I wanted to know what it felt like. Besides, that's what you did in high school; you made out."

From earliest childhood, our young are bombarded with sexual imagery that excites curiosity and stirs the fires within. But the mystery remains. They may speak with a sophistication that sometimes shocks, sometimes reassures the adults around them. But their words belie their naïveté about sex in general and their anxiety about their own sexuality in particular. They know that their bodies are changing, that they are in the throes of an unaccustomed set of emotions and sensations, that sex has something to do with it all. But they're uncertain about just what this means, not even sure about what this thing called "sex" is. "I remember it was right at the beginning of high school and a bunch of us were sitting around bullshitting about sex like kids do," laughed 42-year-old Paul, a Seattle carpenter, whose memory took him back to Baltimore in the late 1950s, "and one of the guys said, 'Hey, wouldn't it be embarrassing if you were getting ready to screw and you suddenly got a hard-on?' "

Such remembrances are not given to the conventional decade of the fifties alone. Those who came to puberty long after the sixties and the onset of the sexual revolution have their own stories of ignorance and bafflement to tell. "There's all this talk about sex all around, but kids don't even know what their bodies will do," exclaimed a 29-year-old Texas geologist with exasperation, as he commented on the paradox of the public talk and the private silence. "The first time I saw semen come out of me, I was scared to death. I thought I broke something, you know, that something had gone wrong with my wiring.

"It sounds funny now, but believe me, I didn't think it was funny then. I was young, about 11, maybe 12 at most. I was playing with myself, but not trying to come; I didn't even know what that was then. All of a sudden I had this strong sensation that I needed to go to the bathroom and then this stuff came shooting out of me. I didn't know what to do. I freaked out. I was afraid to tell my parents because I'd already gotten the message from them that I wasn't supposed to be doing what I was doing. So I just kept quiet and kept worrying and waited to see if something else would come leaking out of my body."

Over three-quarters of the women and nearly all the men in this study masturbated well before their first sexual intercourse, often before their first sexual experience of any kind with another person. The figures for the women are particularly striking when compared with the Kinsey study, which shows that less than 40 percent had masturbated before their first sexual experience, and only a little more than 12 percent had done so to orgasm.[1]

Could some part of this dramatic difference be due to the fact that earlier generations of women felt more shame about this hidden activity, therefore were less willing to speak of it than women are today? Perhaps so. But it isn't likely that this alone can account for such a large difference. Moreover, even this most conservative explanation suggests a change of major proportions both in women's private response to their own sexuality and in the public acceptance of it. For if they couldn't talk then but can now, something has happened in the intervening years that requires explanation.

Enter the sexual revolution of the sixties. Without the continuing liberation of female sexuality, which has been its most significant consequence, change of such magnitude could not have taken place. Nor could the feminist writers and sex therapists who have given encouragement to female masturbation in these last years have been so successful in their efforts.[2]

Yet, although almost everyone is doing it, masturbation remains an activity shrouded in silence. Over and over women and men of all ages spoke of the secrecy that surrounded masturbation in their youth, of their ignorance of what they were doing and of their clear understanding that if the adults around them knew, there would be trouble. Sometimes, this knowledge came to them directly and forcefully, as when a parent caught a child in the act. "I was maybe 6 or 7, and I didn't even think I was doing anything wrong," explained 40-year-old Larry, a Philadelphia architect, shaking his head in wonder as he recalled the scene. "I thought it was like anything else you'd do to make yourself feel good. I didn't know it was a sexual thing; *that* I already knew was something bad. My mother walked into the room and saw what I was doing and had a fit. She grabbed my hand away, then got all flustered and said she didn't ever want to see me doing that again and practically ran out of the room.

A few minutes later, my father came in to have a talk with me. Even then, I knew my mother had sent him because whatever I had done was really bad news."

In other families, the communication is less direct. Parents may be open about a whole range of life experiences, including sex, but masturbation remains the activity that's least likely to be talked about, and even less likely to be named. Children who may witness all kinds of emotional expression and sexual innuendo between their parents never see or hear anything that even suggests that this thing they do is something anyone else knows about, let alone engages in. In such a setting, parents don't have to frown upon the masturbatory activities of a child; they have only to avoid noticing and labeling it for it to become suspect. By singling it out with silence, they send a message that the child interprets to mean that *this* nameless activity is something we don't talk about, one that calls for guilt and concealment.

Consequently, even children who never had any direct experience with parental disapproval nevertheless understood that this was something they'd better keep to themselves. "I was a kid who masturbated from an early age, but I didn't know what to name it, and nobody ever said a word about it," said 33-year-old Marge, a social worker in Santa Cruz, California. "I assumed that I had this magical thing I did to my body and that no one else knew about it. I didn't even know it was sex, even though I would have these erotic fantasies. I fell in love with a cowboy on TV, and he was my amorous pal in my masturbatory fantasies. But I knew not to talk about it and to do it in private where nobody would know."

Even when parents name it and talk to children about masturbation, the child usually gets a message that's perplexing at best. Experts today advise parents to say quietly and calmly that it's all right to masturbate, but only in private, not where anyone can see. But what can a child think when s/he hears these words? If it's all right, why does it have to be hidden? The words and music are out of sync. For children, who are masters at hearing the unspoken message, it's the music that will count more than the words.

Whether met with loud disapproval, deafening silence or seemingly reasonable words, these responses to a child's early masturbatory activities often generate the first conscious moments of conflict about the pleasures of sex—conflict that can help shape the internal experience of sexuality in the years to come. At the beginning, masturbating is nothing more than, as Larry said, "anything else you'd do to make yourself feel good." But the child quickly finds out it isn't so. For some mysterious reason, other "feel good" activities are acceptable, but this one is forbidden. Or, if not actually prohibited, it must be hidden from view, something the child knows not to talk about or to show to another. The meaning, even if never stated explicitly, soon becomes clear: Sex and the feelings it generates are illicit. As a result, not just sex but the pleasure associated with it often becomes tainted by guilt and anxiety—unwelcome feelings that can contaminate adult sexuality when the stirrings of sexual excitement and pleasure re-create the old anxiety about the forbidden.

All this notwithstanding, masturbation generally remains an important and pleasurable sexual activity throughout life, helping to soothe and calm in moments of stress, serving as a repository for sexual fantasies, the place where fantasy life can be experienced with minimum risk or apprehension. For most people, however, by the time the threshold of puberty has been crossed, the main focus of sexual *interest* shifts from the solitary experience to the more social one. It is in the content of the sex play at this time and the age at which it starts that the impact of the sexual revolution becomes most obvious.

Among the older cohort, those over 40 who reached adolescence in the late fifties and early sixties, such experimentation started much later and the limits of acceptable behavior were much more narrowly defined. Laurie, a 43-year-old Los Angeles fashion designer, remembers, "It started around 16, maybe a little later. There was a lot of kissing, touching of breasts, a lot of grinding up against somebody, but no physical hands-on stuff, not until quite a bit later, maybe about 18 or so, when I was already in college.

"This was the late fifties, remember. It was the talk of the school if a girl went much further than that. There was nothing more important to a girl than her 'rep.' It was very delicately balanced, and any sexual stuff that went beyond what was permissible could push a girl over the edge. Believe me, in those days a 'nice' girl didn't worry about things like pregnancy or diseases or anything like that; it was your reputation."

Reputation—a girl's most prized possession in that era, inextricable from her virginity. Her "good name," she was reminded in a hundred ways, was all she had, her ticket to a respectable marriage and a place in the community. For this thing called "rep" not only determined the kind of relationships a girl would have with boys in high school, it was her most important bargaining chip in her search for a proper husband.

It didn't make any difference whether a girl had, in fact, "gone all the way"; it was what people thought that counted. So deeply internalized were these sexual constraints and the concerns about "rep" that it's still possible, a quarter of a century later, to evoke those old feelings in women of that generation. Shaking her head in disbelief, 44-year-old Joan, an administrator at Stanford University, told of a recent lunch with two friends during which the three women fell to trading stories of high-school experiences. "I was telling them about this boyfriend I had and talked about making love with him, and Fran, one of my friends, looked surprised and said, 'You mean you actually fucked in high school?' Before I could even think about what was happening, I snapped back at her, 'No, of course we didn't.' I was so surprised at myself; I answered her as if I were still that teenager whose life depended on people understanding that I was one of the good girls. It was really crazy; it threw me right back to those years and all the feelings I had then."

It was different for the girls and the boys, of course, at least as far as what was permissible. The boys claimed experience they didn't have; the girls feigned naïveté even when they were sexually knowledgeable. It wasn't just the boys they worried about, however. Rather, acceptance by the other girls, an acceptance whose importance at this age transcended any concern about relations with boys, required adherence to the sexual rules of the day. For although the rules may have been made by someone else, they were internalized by the girls who assumed responsibility for policing them, often more rigorously than anyone outside the peer group. Therefore, violations were kept secret, often even from best friends, and the girl prayed the boy wouldn't talk.

An interesting phenomenon this, acted upon especially forcefully in the sexual arena. Women police each other to make certain that male rules about female behavior are not violated. Why? Partly because, as the old adage says, and the mothers of these teenagers surely warned them, "We're known by the company we keep." In the fifties, certainly, to be in the company of a girl who was labeled "fast" was to damage one's own reputation as well.

Undoubtedly, also, the same girls who sat in judgment on others were struggling with their own unruly sexual feelings, trying to separate themselves from them, to put them on hold until the socially approved moment arrived. What better way to deny these feelings that were so threatening than to externalize them and project them onto others? In the process they could reinforce their belief that they were different from those others, better, more truly the epitome of desirable feminine virtue.

But to know it for oneself was not enough. The knowledge had to be public to be convincing on the inside and effective on the outside. Only when the world knew and affirmed them in this could they feel secure that the promised prizes of womanhood would be theirs; only then could they feel sure of both the acceptance of women and the admiration of men.

While the rules of teenage dating and the exigencies of the marriage market are compelling explanations in themselves, other powerful forces play their part in making girls and women into the enforcers of female virtue. Among them, none is more significant than the phenomenon of identification with the aggressor, a common occurrence among individuals in any powerless group. It's this that helps to explain the behavior of the black police in South Africa, of the colonial Indians who adopted English manners and mores, of the Jewish police in the Nazi death camps, and of the girls and women of whom I have been speaking.

By identifying with the powerful, the disempowered achieve a measure of safety, at least for a moment. By doing the bidding of those in power, they become a necessary part of the system, useful so long as they serve to contain the stirrings and strivings of the oppressed. By making the rules and values of their oppressor their own, they separate themselves from the rest of their group and, temporarily at least, assuage the pain of their stigmatized status.

For the teenage girls of the fifties, all these pressures came together to give the peer-group norms extraordinary force. "Any girl would lie about it if she went beyond what the other girls thought was okay. That was the worst, when the girls found out that somebody let a guy get to third base or, God forbid, if she let him do IT. So if you did anything like that, you hoped and prayed they'd never know," explained 46-year-old Sue Ann, a housewife and mother in suburban Detroit.

All too often, however, it was a vain hope, since the rules that guided the boys' behavior were just the opposite. Just as a girl's "rep" rested on being a virtuous maiden, a boy's was tied to being a macho stud. To be an accepted part of the peer group, a boy had to invent experiences even when he had none. Status, prestige, his very sense of himself and his masculinity were at stake. The more experience he could claim, the more conquests he could brag about, the more important he appeared in the eyes of others, therefore in his own. It was almost inevitable, then, that when he actually did "make it" with a girl, he would talk.

"At least 50 percent of my wanting to be with a girl had to do with impressing the guys; I didn't want to be ridiculed and laughed at," said a 40-year-old Memphis accountant ruefully, as he felt once again the pain of that period of his life. "I mean, sure I wanted a girlfriend; I wanted that experience, you know, to know what it was all about. But what made it really imperative was wanting to be one of the guys. It's as simple as that.

"I don't know how much lying went on then, but I know there was plenty because I did it, too. All those kids bragging about how they were making it with some girl. Well, you want to be one of them, so you make up stories about how you got to touch a girl's tits even if you didn't get near them."

By the time most of the over-40s graduated to what they called "heavy petting," which for them meant genital fondling, they were either out of high school or well on their way to graduation. Obviously, there were some who were sexually precocious, boys and girls who violated the mores of their time. But in a culture where most high-school girls cherished their virginity, most boys had no choice but to remain virginal as well. For those who did not, it usually meant "fooling around with one of *those* girls, the sluts," as one 45-year-old man said. For the girls who were labeled thus, it could be devastating. Their reputation in shreds, they were cast out of respectable peer society, sometimes even forced to leave school because of the notoriety that surrounded them. Yet some of the women who told such stories swore that they had not even "gone all the way."

Forty-three-year-old Maureen, a social worker in Cleveland, could barely contain her tears as she recalled the anguish she felt then. "I was a lonely kid, not very outgoing or popular, and my mother worried about that a lot, kept after me, I mean. I guess she'd been Miss Popularity when she was a kid and wanted me to be like her. But I wasn't. The way she carried on, I felt like I'd failed in life by the time I was 10. So when I got to high school and the kids began to play around sexually, I found out that was one way to be popular.

"I don't want you to think I did anything so terrible; I mean, I didn't fuck or anything like that. But I made out with a lot of guys, a lot of heavy petting, very heavy. And guys talk. They lied, too, and said more happened than really did. I knew they were lying because each time I'd be with a new guy, he'd be surprised when I wouldn't let him go all the way.

"By the time I was in the eleventh grade, nobody would hardly talk to me except for the guys who wanted to get in my pants. God, I was miserable. In the middle of that year, I refused to go back to school. I stayed out the rest of eleventh grade, and my parents sent me to a shrink. Then, after that, they sent me away to an all-girls school for the rest of high school."

Generally, the script between young people of that generation called for the boys to try and for the girls to find ways to foil their attempts, or at least to play hard-to-get convincingly. But the whole dance took place in the context of a peculiar and perverse sexual dynamic in which the girls were expected to be both sexually alluring and virginal at one and the same time. They had to be sexy to be popular, a virgin to be marriageable. "It wasn't just that we were pushy, aggressive boys and they were sweet little resisting girls," insisted a 44-year-old Albany professor as he described the sexual ethos of the day. "The girls were seductive as hell. The way they dressed was a come on— tight skirts that showed off their asses and bras that made their breasts so pointy they practically hit you in the face. But when it came right down to it, it was, 'Look, but don't touch.' We had a name for those girls: cock-teasers.

"When I look back now, I can see that the girls were in a hell of a bind. They were damned if they did and pretty lonely if they didn't. They had to walk a very fine line and play it exactly right." Laughing, "I have to admit, a lot of them had the routine down pat. They managed to leave us guys panting plenty."

For both girls and boys, this was a provocative, aggravating and unsatisfying sexual game. Nevertheless, the different norms about male and female sexuality gave the boys a distinct edge, and the age-old issue of conquest was rarely far from their minds. "The whole game was to get a girl to give out," recalled 42-year-old Joel, a New York building contractor. "You expected her to resist; she had to if she wasn't going to ruin her reputation. But you kept pushing. Part of it was the thrill of touching and being touched, but I've got to admit, part of it was conquest, too, and what you'd tell the guys at school the next day."

Why is this male behavior so ubiquitous across class, race,

even across the generations? What is it that makes sexual conquest so central to masculine identity, that makes the erect penis a validation of self? Why is it that so many men equate sexual potency with the "essence of manhood"?[3]

Certainly, there are social forces at play here. The equation of maleness with conquest, aggression, initiation and mastery is as old as time. Clearly, also, the historical moment makes some difference. This was the decade of the fifties, the years of reaction against the difficulties of the thirties and forties—the one featuring the Great Depression, the other dominated by World War II. In the quest for normality once again, gender differences and role divisions were not only accepted as the givens of everyday life, but idealized and acclaimed as the emblems of the good life. And nowhere was the gender dance more elaborately choreographed, the divisions more sharply delineated, than in the sexual arena.

But important as such social realities may be in creating a climate that encourages and legitimates male conquest and aggression, these alone cannot explain why they so persistently manifest themselves in the sexual domain. Without question, the structure of roles and relationships within which we live defines who we are, how we relate to our sexuality, even how we experience sex, in pervasive and powerful ways. But the consistency of the differences between men and women, whether in their sexual responses or in many other of life's arenas, suggests that what is born in the structure of social relationships ultimately emerges as psychological reality with a life and force of its own.

To understand how this works to create the kind of male sexual behavior I have been talking about, we must take a short excursion into the psychology of infancy. In the matter of identity, whether male or female, no institution in our society is more important than the family.[4] For it is there that our identity finds its first expression, there that it is shaped and molded by our earliest attachments and identifications. Other events, the experiences of later years, changing standards of masculinity and femininity—all these influence the development of a personal identity, of course. But they are laid down on the foundation of our initial experiences in the family—experiences that are driven into our unconscious, and remain there to become the filter through which later events and circumstances are understood and interpreted.

From the beginning, life is a process of forming attachments and making identifications with significant people from the external world. Since mother usually is the primary caregiver of infancy, it is she with whom we make our first attachment, she with whom we identify as one like self. Other connections, internalizations and identifications may have been made during the early months of life—with father, siblings, grandparents, babysitters. But so long as mother has been the primary caretaker, it is she who remains the object of the most important attachment and earliest identification for children of both genders.

As infancy passes, the process of separation and individuation begins. This involves, among other things, the need to develop an independent and coherent sense of self. Central to this developmental stage are the crystallization of a gender identity and the maintenance of what psychologists call "ego boundaries"— those personal psychological boundaries that set us off from the rest of the world. This, in large part, is what a child's separation struggle is all about—a struggle to incorporate a personal identity that's unique and autonomous, to develop an "I" that stands separate and apart from the "You."

For a girl, the establishment of a gender identity is direct and continuous, the consolidation of an identification with mother that has been in place since the first days of life. But for a boy, it's a demanding and painful process that means a profound upheaval in his internal world. For in order to identify with his maleness, he must renounce his primary identification with mother and shift it instead to an appropriate male object. In doing so, he not only repudiates the feminine in himself, but develops a set of ego boundaries that are fixed and firm—protective defenses that rigidly separate self from other, that keep him distant from his own emotional life as well as from the kind of intimate connection that might leave him vulnerable to experiencing again the pain and loss of this early separation.

How can a small child make sense of the need for such a radical shift in his inner life? How can he make this demand that feels so *un*reasonable seem reasonable? Anatomy helps. He has a penis; mother does not. *This* is what makes him different; *this* is what makes this painful task necessary. *This*, therefore, is what defines his identity, his maleness. Yet it's a fragile definition, resting as it does on the renunciation of the female rather than on the direct and positive incorporation of the male. It's this shift, I believe, that is at least partly responsible for the fear of impotence, both actual and metaphorical, that blights male consciousness, a fear that's made manifest by the concern, so often expressed in folk culture, about the "fragile male ego."

The deprivation a boy experiences in having to relinquish his early identification with mother is complicated by the Oedipal issues that arise around age 3 or 4. The effort to forswear his forbidden sexual desires for mother, his fear of the competition with father and the consequent castration anxiety, are laid over the earlier issues of identification, separation and individuation.[5] Together, they explain a great deal about the aggressiveness that's said to be so natural in men. When directed against women, we can understand it as a response to these early losses and to the sense of betrayal that went with them. For the child's inner experience is not that he did something, but that something was done to him—that this mother who had, until then, been the loved adult on whom he could count, with whom he could identify, abandoned him to the shadowy and alien world of men. How, then, could she, or any woman, ever be wholly trusted again?

Whether true in the literal sense or not is irrelevant; it's the way the experience is internalized and understood by the child that counts. In this sense, the need for such repression engenders feelings of abandonment that are, in themselves, enough to stimulate plenty of rage. But it seems to me that we are witness also to a case of aggression turned outward in an attempt to compensate for the original aggression that was turned inward when, as a small child, he had to sunder his inner life so ruthlessly.

Parenthetically, it's in this developmental sequence that we can make sense of the contempt for women we see so often among men. If we consider the dilemma of the small boy and the internal rupture this separation requires, we can understand that the contempt is born of fear, not arrogance—the fear of a child who finds himself pressed to reject so powerful an inner presence as mother has been in his early life. It's a fear so great that he can live with it only by disempowering her—by convincing himself that she's a weak and puny creature whose lack of maleness must doom her forever to a subordinate and contemptible place in the world.

Seen from this vantage point, the seemingly unremitting search for sexual conquest is more complicated than it looks. Partly it's an attempt at mastery and control, an unconscious need to rework the old traumatic experience with a woman, to give it a different ending. He leaves; he isn't left. As he moves from woman to woman as conqueror, he ritually and symbolically punishes mother and simultaneously reassures himself that he need never again be fearful of her abandonment.

Partly, also, the drive for sexual conquest is an attempt to recapture the early union with mother. For while we can repress such early connections and the wishes and needs they stir, we cannot undo them. Instead, they are pushed into the unconscious, where they will arise to demand a hearing another day. Thus, the very repudiation of that early connection leaves him forever vulnerable, forever searching to re-create that union with a woman while, at the same time, he remains guarded and untrusting, fearful of being cast out again. When he enters a woman sexually, he finds again the bliss he once knew, the depth of feeling and connection he needs. But the very intensity of the feelings becomes a threat from which he must flee, for it constitutes an assault on the boundaries between self and other he erected so long ago. So he leaves, only to begin the search again soon thereafter.

A question arises: Have the changing prescriptions about masculinity had some effect? The answer is mixed. If we're looking for signs of major change, then it's an unequivocal no. But if we'll settle for less, there are hopeful glimmerings of such possibilities in some of the younger men, those in their late teens and early twenties. Not many, to be sure, but a few, who seem less rigidly bound, more concerned with the quality of the relationship than with the sexual posturing that's so prevalent among the older men.

Undoubtedly the loosening of the masculine stereotype set in motion by the feminist movement has been important in this development. But only when fathers share the care of the infant from birth onward will male identity formation proceed without the kind of wrenching shift I have been describing. Then a boy will internalize a primary identification with father as well as mother and, because there will be no discontinuity for him to contend with, adult male identity will be more resilient and more multifaceted. But until a male figure is an active presence in the inner life of the male infant, the changes in the culture will have only limited effect.

As each generation has passed through these years before the big IT, the initiation into sexual activity has come at younger and younger ages, and the meaning of "everything but" has been modified and the content broadened. Among the older generation, the range of acceptable behaviors was narrow, and the rules about what a girl could do, how far she could go in her sexual explorations, clear and unequivocal. The younger age groups, however, have become progressively more permissive and less judgmental about those who violate the norms of the day. It isn't that the good girl–bad girl distinctions are gone from their world or that concern for reputation no longer exists. But the boundary of the unacceptable continues to recede, and behaviors that were almost unheard of yesterday have become commonplace today.

Take oral sex, for example. Among the men and women now over 40, less than one-tenth had any experience with it before they'd had sexual intercourse and, of those, very few tried it in high school. For them, too, oral sex almost always meant fellatio, both women and men agreeing that, if they thought of it at all then, the idea of cunnilingus seemed very unappealing. But for most of this generation, neither was much of an option in those early years.

"Oral sex? In those days? Are you kidding? I can't even imagine any of the girls I knew getting into that then."

"Oral sex? No, that was an invention of college, and after I was already screwing around. I don't know if any of the guys thought about it much then. I don't think the thought even crossed my mind in high school, at least I don't remember it if it did."

"I saw an old high-school boyfriend of mine a few years ago, and I asked him why we didn't ever fuck or suck. He laughed and said, 'I don't know; girls didn't do things like that in the fifties.' "

Typical replies from those who grew up then. For the boys who deviated from this norm, there were no problems. But for the girls, there was shame and blame. "I remember doing it because this guy I liked so much wanted me to, but I couldn't look at myself in the mirror after that. I felt so dirty; it was awful."

"Ugh, I did it because I was a dumb jerk. I thought I was in love, and I wanted him in my life so desperately. It didn't work. He took one of those nice, goody-goody girls to his senior prom. He married her a couple of years later, too."

With each succeeding generation, the incidence of both cunnilingus and fellatio goes up, although the latter continues to be the more frequent. By way of explanation, some of the women spoke of "logistics." "Just think about it," insisted 25-year-old Karen, a secretary in Atlanta. "You're in a car and it's hard to move around. Logistically, he's more accessible, that's all. It was a lot easier to give him head than for him to go down on me."

But, of course, there are other reasons as well, reasons that are rooted in the aversion to women's genitals—to the taste, the smell, the fear that they're unclean. The women's movement made a difference, it's true. The celebration of "woman as beautiful," the understanding and acceptance of the fact that cunnilingus is very often the way women reach orgasm most easily, the new sexual assertiveness wherein women expect reciprocity in oral sex—all these have made both women and men more open to cunnilingus now than ever before. Still, the old inhibitions are not completely gone, and people of all generations spoke of feeling them keenly, especially in these early years of sexual experimentation. "At the time, it seemed so intimate and, I don't know, dark, not clean enough, maybe," remarked 32-year-old Becky, a housewife and mother of two small children in Tucson.

"I couldn't even think about it then; it seemed dirty, revolting," recalled her husband, Dan, a 35-year-old electrician.

Statistically, the proportion of people who experienced oral sex in one form or another at this stage rises to almost one-fifth for those in their thirties and to over one-quarter among the 20–29s. In this latter group, when the college students are separated out and examined alone, the incidence climbs once again, this time to close to one-half.[6]

As the barriers fall and cunnilingus and fellatio become a more common part of the "everything but" years, they take on considerably less significance in the minds and hearts of the young people who do them. Few of the younger groups, those who were born between the mid-sixties and mid-seventies and are now in their teens and early twenties, said they never thought about it. Quite the contrary. It's a common enough experience to be known and understood as a sexual option, even among those who choose not to exercise it; common enough, too, to generate a high level of curiosity. "People are always talking about blow jobs, and I'd never done it because I always kind of thought it was yichhh, you know, yucky," said Rebecca, a 16-year-old from Chicago, her face screwed up in a gesture of distaste. "But I was curious about it, so one night I was out with this guy I like, and he was pushing me to have sex and I didn't want to so I gave him a blow job instead. It was kind of fun, like sucking on a lollypop."

In an earlier book, published in 1976, I wrote that oral sex

was resisted by many of the young married women I interviewed.[7] In response, I received a half dozen letters from prostitutes around the country telling me that this was why married
men came to them. "Every married guy who comes in here
wants to stick it in my mouth because their wives won't let
them," wrote one of the prostitutes. Once, men had to go to
prostitutes to get oral sex; now, it's "fun, like sucking on a lollypop"—a vivid illustration of the shift in sexual norms, taste
and sensibility in an astonishingly short time.

Parenthetically, the statute books still describe oral sex as
"sodomy," a practice that remains illegal in twenty-four states
and the District of Columbia.[8] True, these laws are enforced
only very rarely, and then usually selectively against homosex-
uals, as in the case of the Georgia man whose conviction for
sodomy, performed in his own bedroom, was upheld by the U.S.
Supreme Court.[9] Nevertheless, they remain on the books—a
reminder that it wasn't long ago when this behavior, which,
among heterosexuals, has now been demoted to logistics and
birthday presents, was such a deeply felt taboo that it was made
illegal.[10]

Most, although certainly not all, of the young people who
engaged in oral sex did so in the context of an ongoing relationship. For them, it was an ordinary part of the sexual exploration
of these years. Teenagers spoke of giving and getting "blow jobs,"
of "giving head," of "going down" on each other with an ease
that would astonish the over-35s. The same kids fended off questions about feelings and meanings with a shrug and one version
or another of "It's no big deal." But as the conversation went
on, it became clear that, while it may not have been a "big"
deal, it was some kind of a deal for a significant number of girls
at least.

For some, performing fellatio was the only way they could get
what they wanted sexually. "I like it when he goes down on me,
but I don't really like putting that big thing in my mouth. I feel
like I'm going to choke sometimes," said Diana, a 16-year-old
from Raleigh, North Carolina. "But it's only fair; if I want it, I
have to do it, too."

For others, fellatio was a way of staving off intercourse for a while longer. "I was a sophomore in high school, and I had a boyfriend I was crazy about. After we were going together for a month or so, things moved into oral sex," said Bonnie, a 19-year-old sales clerk from Portland, Oregon.

"Why oral sex and not intercourse?" I asked.

With a shrug, she answered, "It was your virginity you were saving; anything else was okay. So if you were with someone, you'd give him a blow job but not intercourse. It's hard to think about that now, I mean, getting that intimate and still caring about actual penetration. But then it made a difference."

"Did you enjoy it?"

"I don't think I thought much about it," she replied. "I guess I didn't like it, but I didn't *not* like it either. It was something he wanted, and it took care of him. I guess sex at that time was geared to getting him off. I mean, I enjoyed what we did; I loved being close to him. But I was so young, and I was really afraid he'd push me into having sex if I didn't do it."

"I was afraid he'd push me into having sex." Interesting, isn't it, the hold virginity still has on us. Why is it that we break all the other sexual rules before this one? What meaning does it really have? Most obvious, of course, is the fact that in our society a woman's value still is not wholly divorced from her virginity. We're looser about it than ever before, it's true. But even now, we're not without a great deal of ambivalence, which we see reflected in the fight over abortion, in the continuing attempts to dismantle family-planning programs and in the demand that sex-education programs emphasize celibacy.

The fear of pregnancy is an issue as well, of course. But given the available birth-control options now, it hardly seems reason enough to forestall intercourse after so many other sexual behaviors have been acted on for so long. Moreover, most girls and young women today know they'll have sexual intercourse long before they're ready to bear children. So the question remains: Why is it less anxiety-provoking to have a penis in the mouth than in the vagina?

Partly, I believe, the answer lies in the social definitions of the body itself, in the way these define our relationship to its various parts and in the symbolic meaning we attach to each of them. The mouth is visible, accessible, a part of the body in constant, everyday use. We open it, speak with it, touch it, brush it, put our fingers in it, explore it with our tongue. Symbolically the mouth is public, part of our face to the world, central to our presentation of self. But the vagina is private. We don't use it, can't see it, rarely ever touch it, usually don't put our fingers inside it, even when masturbating. It's an invisible, dark, shadowy, mysterious place—a secret place that no one enters, one we know little or nothing about.

Perhaps because of its hidden nature, perhaps because it's so close to the place where the body excretes its wastes, perhaps because of its relationship to the birth process, the cultural imagery around the vagina has been highly ambivalent, reflecting disgust and dread on the one hand and the promise of life on the other—the *vagina dentata* as opposed to the all-giving, all-powerful mother; the precious, sacred place that's also smelly and unclean. Confusing and frightening imagery for all of us. And for all too many women, shameful as well.

For a man, such images can become a challenge, an invitation to enter, to conquer. For a woman, however, entry can stir some deeply felt fear, a sense of violation, of encroachment on her body's boundaries. It's this sense of invasion that may explain why a woman so often avoids the sexual encounter—a common complaint in marriages—even when she also acknowledges that she finds it gratifying and pleasurable once she gets involved.[11] For the young and sexually uninitiated, then, fellatio may be easier to handle emotionally than sexual intercourse, since it doesn't threaten the integrity of the body, doesn't trespass on any sacred terrain.

There's little doubt that over the course of the last two and a half decades very large changes have taken place in the pre-intercourse sexual behavior of the young. It's true that most boys and girls still are locked in a giving-getting struggle, he pushing her for as much as he can get, she holding out for as little as she can give. And it's also true that girls still worry about maintaining their virginity, just as they did before. But now they face the problem at 15 instead of 20—not just a simple five-year-difference but the difference between a child and a young adult.

What happened in each generation when people took the next step, and how they felt about it when they did, is our next concern as we move now to look at "the first time."

---

1. Alfred C. Kinsey et al., *Sexual Behavior in the Human Female* (Philadelphia: W. B. Saunders, 1953). The Kinsey figures are not directly comparable but must be computed. To do so, I have taken his data, which show that only 18 percent of the 18-year-old women in his sample had had sexual intercourse (see p. 286, Figure 43), and compared this with his figure for masturbation at the same age (see p. 141, Figure 9).

2. See, for example, Lonnie Barbach, *For Yourself: The Fulfillment of Female Sexuality* (Garden City, N.Y.: Doubleday Anchor, 1976), and the more recent book by Betty Dodson, *Sex for One: The Joy of Selfloving* (New York: Harmony Books, 1988).

3. See Lillian B. Rubin, *Intimate Strangers: Men and Women Together* (New York: Harper Perennial Library, 1984), Chapter 5.

4. For a fuller exposition of this theoretical perspective, see Nancy Chodorow, *The Reproduction of Mothering* (Berkeley: University of California Press, 1978); Dorothy Dinnerstein, *The Mermaid and the Minotaur* (New York: Harper & Row, 1976); and Lillian B. Rubin, *Intimate Strangers: Men and Women Together* (New York: Harper Perennial Library, 1984), Chapters 3 and 5.

5. Those who subscribe to classical psychoanalytic theory will argue that this accounting doesn't attend sufficiently to the whole issue of infantile sexuality, of the sexual desires the infant and small boy has for his mother and of the Oedipal crisis through which he must pass as he renounces those impulses. I do not deny the importance of those impulses and desires in the formation of male sexuality and, even more important, in men's later sexual relations with women. Nor do I think we need to make a choice between these two theoretical perspectives. My argument, however, is that long before the Oedipal issues and castration anxiety make themselves felt, the process of dealing with the pre-Oedipal issues of identification, separation and individuation has already made its mark on the development of children of both genders. Moreover, unlike classical Freudian theorists, I do not believe that the resolution of the Oedipus

conflict settles the issue of identity or sexuality for all time. Rather, like most developmental theorists, I see the formation of identity—in all its aspects, including sexual—as much more complex, more fluid, and capable of change and modification throughout all of life.

6. Among whites, the college-educated are more likely than those with a high-school education or less to have more liberal sexual attitudes and to be more sexually experimental. The difference, then, is due to the fact that about 30 percent of those interviewed were working-class men and women who had never gone beyond high school.

7. Lillian Breslow Rubin, *Worlds of Pain: Life in the Working-Class Family* (New York: Basic/Harper Torchbook, 1976), Chapter 8.

8. Technically, sodomy is defined in the law as "placing in contact the genitals of one individual against the mouth or anus of another individual."

9. See *Bowers* v. *Hardwick*, 106 S.Ct. 2841 (1986).

10. In upholding the sodomy conviction in *Bowers*, the majority turned to the history of sodomy laws and wrote in part: "Sodomy was a criminal offense at common law and was forbidden by the laws of the original thirteen states when they ratified the Bill of Rights. In 1868, when the Fourteenth Amendment was ratified, all but 5 of the 37 states in the Union had criminal sodomy laws. In fact, until 1961, all 50 states outlawed sodomy" (p. 2845).

11. For a more detailed discussion, see Rubin, *Intimate Strangers*, p. 111.

# 3

## The First Time

"*I* was 15. I'd never seen an erect penis before, so I got really scared. I thought: 'Oh my God, that's never going to fit inside me,' " said Marian, a 29-year-old sales clerk in Boston, who laughed at herself as she recalled her first time. "But then I figured since that's how you do it, it must work."

"How did you feel about it?" I asked.

"I knew I was supposed to be losing something valuable, my virginity, and I guess I was ambivalent. I was worried because I'd heard that men wanted to marry virgins, and I worried that if the person I wanted to marry knew I wasn't a virgin, he wouldn't marry me. The whole thing was a mess, because where I grew up and went to school, a girl was a snob if she didn't and a whore if she did."

For men, too, the first time is fraught with fears and anxieties, although different from those of the women. "I was in the tenth grade and had this job in this fast-food restaurant after school. This girl came in one day and we started talking, just fooling around. She hung around until I finished my shift, then we went out and went back to her house. Her parents weren't there, so we started making out, and I knew it was going to happen. I was scared at first; I was afraid I wouldn't know what to do or I'd do something wrong," said Ben, a 25-year-old graduate student at the University of Chicago.

"And did you?" I asked.

With a smile, "No, it seemed to be the most natural and easy thing in the world, and I didn't understand why I was so afraid before. I didn't know why everyone thought it was so great, though. It seemed kind of overrated. But it was funny because, even though I didn't know what was so great about it, I felt as if I should want to get it as often as possible after that. I guess that's because, if you're a guy, you're supposed to want it."

Only about one-tenth of the men and women in this study used words of pleasure to describe their first time. A few of the men actually enjoyed the sex itself. "It was fantastic, great. I thought this could become addictive," said 40-year-old Orin, a San Francisco lawyer, whose first time was at 20. But for most of them, it was the *idea* that gave so much pleasure, not the act itself. "It was wonderful. Finally I knew what the mystery and restrictions were all about. It was an incredible feeling, like crossing the great divide," enthused 28-year-old Darrell, a statistician from Phoenix. "Not the sex per se but just knowing what it was all about, getting past that barrier. It was a great feeling, something to remember."

Among the women who spoke positively of their first time, it was almost always with someone they had known and cared about for some time before, usually a man who was somewhat older and more experienced. "It was wonderful," said 24-year-old Judy, a computer programmer in Los Angeles. "It was the summer before my senior year of high school, so I guess I was 17. I was a holdout for that era."

"What was wonderful about it?" I asked.

"Everything. The timing was right; it was with a guy I had known for years and had a crush on for a long time. And he was several years older than me, so he was quite experienced. He knew what he was doing, and he was tender and caring and loving. Also, I knew that it wasn't going to be the last time I'd see him. That's what happened to so many of my friends, and I didn't want it to be like that for me. So it felt really good to be doing it with him."

Most people, however, described their first time with words like "overrated," "disappointing," "a waste," "awful," "boring," "stupid," "empty," "ridiculous," "awkward," "miserable," "un-memorable." But the interpretation of the event, the meaning it had, was very different for men and for women. No matter what their age, the men construed it in the context of our social definitions of masculinity. They talked about "crossing a great divide," said they felt a "burden was lifted," the "pressure was off," a "hurdle was gotten over." They characterized the expe-rience as an "important accomplishment," a "landmark achieve-ment." For them, it was a rite of passage, a crucial step on the road to manhood—a step in which they exulted, even if they didn't fully enjoy the experience itself. "It was a great relief," said 32-year-old Mark, a New York dentist. "I didn't feel like it made me a man exactly, but it was one hell of an important step. It meant more in terms of what could now happen as opposed to the experience itself, which wasn't much of anything. I felt like I had entered a whole new world of real grown-up sex. I said before it didn't exactly make me a man, but it meant I had entered the world of men. And *that* was a very heady experience for me."

For some men, it was the conquest that was memorable. "I didn't like her especially, but she was the prettiest girl in the class," recalled 40-year-old Chuck, a TV cameraman from Den-ver. "It was a notch rather than anything else, and that's what I did for some years afterward—collected notches."

For others, the knowledge that their accomplishment would impress their friends was at least as important as the sexual encounter itself. "It wasn't romantic; I didn't know what the hell I was doing," exclaimed a 25-year-old Santa Fe cook, a look of disgust crossing his face as he recalled the feelings he had then. "You're more scared than enjoying it, and more concerned with how to do it than with getting that good feeling that intercourse can provide. I mean, I was excited, but not at all in control. It went so quickly, it's almost like it didn't happen. But you'd never know any of that from the way the guys talked about it. And I was just like the rest of them, I'm ashamed to say, talking it up and telling everyone how great it was. What a crock!"

In the aftermath of the first time, then, whatever disappointment the men suffered was overshadowed by the exhilaration of the achievement, of having crossed over into the world of men. For the women, however, the experience had a different set of meanings, complicated as it was by the social ambivalence about women's sexuality and by important generational differences in what was considered acceptable sexual behavior.

Among the over-35s—those who came to adolescence between the early 1950s and the mid-1960s—the mandate about virginity and the fear of pregnancy were live issues that had to be resolved before the women could act. No matter what their class or status, therefore, sexual activity generally started later than for those who came after them. Within this group, however, there also were differences.

For the women who had no college plans, the first experience with sexual intercourse usually came substantially earlier than for their college-bound sisters, in the eleventh or twelfth grade when they were about 16 or 17. "It was sort of known in the school that the college-prep kids didn't, or at least the girls didn't, and then there were the rest of us," said 41-year-old Gladys, a postal clerk in Pittsburgh. "I don't mean that *everybody* else did, but my friends did, and I did, too. I started having sex with my boyfriend in the twelfth grade. I was lucky; I didn't get caught. But a lot of the girls did, and they had to get married. You couldn't get an abortion then; no one even thought about it."

In the culture of the times, getting pregnant generally meant getting married. With no career at stake, with a future that generally meant some small job until they could marry and have children, getting pregnant didn't seem as risky to these girls as it did to those who were college-bound.[1] "I can't think of a girl who got pregnant in my high school who didn't get married," said 37-year-old Don, an urban planner who grew up in Arkansas. "I suppose there must have been exceptions, but I never knew about them, and all the guys I knew just assumed if that happened they'd have to marry her."

For the women who expected to continue their education, the first time generally occurred after they were in college. "I'd never have taken a chance in high school because I didn't want to ruin my life. I knew I wanted to go to college, and I just couldn't risk it, getting pregnant, I mean," said 45-year-old Lila, a psychologist from Cleveland.

Obviously, it wasn't only the fear of spoiling plans for college that restrained girls like Lila in high school. The social stigma attached to an unmarried pregnancy, the personal shame and family disgrace that would accompany it, the wrath of parents— all these were enough to make a girl of any class proceed with caution. My point, however, is that when college plans were added to the picture, it became another factor to be reckoned with, another reason for sexual caution.

By the mid- to late sixties, when the women who are now over 35 were arriving on campuses around the country, the sexual revolution had already begun, and the pressures were great to end their virginal state. This was a time when sex became the focus of attention, the topic of the day, as young people struggled against the old constraints without yet being able to formulate and institutionalize a more acceptable set of sexual norms. "Why does sex have to be anything more than a handshake?" they asked defiantly. "It's no big deal," they insisted stoutly.

It wasn't just external social pressure at work, but internal psychological ones as well, for the two are inextricably interwoven. Thus, as women increasingly found themselves in settings that gave legitimacy to their sexual desires, there were internal pressures to satisfy them, just as there had always been for men. But even for those women who continued to have some doubts and anxieties about becoming sexually active, the emerging sexual culture played a powerful role in their decision making. For the need was great to be one with the generation, to belong, not to be left behind.

Wherever they turned, on or off the college campus, sex and sexuality were in the air. Women were making sexual decisions and, more important, talking about them openly in ways that would have seemed impossible just a few years earlier. "Sex was the big thing we talked about all the time in the dorms," said 41-year-old Claire, a clothing buyer in Boston. "It was 1966 and '67, remember. I think most of the girls on the floor had already had sex, and I felt out of it when they talked. So even though I was scared, I was feeling like I *had* to know what it was all about. It was time."

"It was time"—a refrain women of all ages expressed repeatedly. Time for what? Time to end the mystery, to know, to be rid of a burden. Overnight, it seemed, virginity was transformed from a treasure to be safeguarded to a problem to be solved. It didn't happen overnight, of course. Such great social changes never do, even though when we're living through them they seem to come upon us with a suddenness that's astonishing. Rather, we had been moving toward the sexual revolution of the sixties since the early part of the century.

The bohemians of the teens set the stage for the upheaval of the twenties. The decade of the thirties was quieter, preoccupied as it was with the problems of the Great Depression. But it was also a period when the gains of the twenties were consolidated and diffused throughout the society, a time when the behaviors of college students that had shocked the nation a few years earlier were incorporated into the life of the high school.[2] Then came the forties and World War II. The romance of the uniform, the danger, the fear and the loneliness that pervaded the atmosphere of the time all served to loosen the sexual fetters yet another notch.[3] In the aftermath of the war, the fifties were again a quiet decade. But by then the question of whether women were sexually responsive had been fully settled. While premarital virginity was still idealized, doing "everything but" had become a routine part of the dating and mating rituals. And once married, women were expected to turn into eager sexual mates.

Each of these periods liberated women's sexuality, first by recognizing its existence, then by legitimating the premarital sexual experimentation we have come to know so well in this century. It was the revolution of the sixties, however, that smashed the virginity mandate and left it lying in the dust of a time gone by. Until then, a girl went "all the way" at her peril. Suddenly, she felt embattled when she did not. Suddenly, "it was time."

For many of the women who entered college in the sixties, therefore, having intercourse for the first time was a calculated decision. For some, the transition was a relatively easy one, partly at least because they had, for some years, been engaged in the struggle to separate themselves from the established code of sexual behavior and to define their sexuality in ways that seemed more personally fitting. "I was one of those technical virgins where I did 'everything but' from the time I was about 15," said 40-year-old Gloria, a Durham, North Carolina high-school teacher. "Even then I was beginning to question the sexual values I'd been brought up with. I was aware of my own desires very early, and although I felt guilty about them, I couldn't see any reason why boys could have those desires satisfied and girls couldn't. By the time I got to college in 1966, I knew it was time to lay my virginity to rest. And I did, with the first guy I got involved with in my freshman year."

For those who had more fully internalized the sexual rules with which they had been raised, the transition took longer and was made with greater difficulty. But even these women sounded the "it was time" theme. "I had been thinking about it for a long time, but it wasn't until the end of my sophomore year in college that I finally decided it was time I joined the sexual revolution," said 39-year-old Jean, a Washington, D.C., government worker. "Even though my boyfriend and I had been going together for over a year and were making out pretty heavily, I was still worried about whether he'd think less of me once we did the real thing. But I knew it was time; I couldn't hold out much longer."

It wasn't the girls alone for whom college orientation made a difference, however. For the boys who planned to go to college, the first time also often came later than for those who expected to enter the world of work immediately after high school. But the line that divided the college from the noncollege was more blurred for boys than for girls. For the boys, there was neither the stigma nor the immediate personal consequences of a potential pregnancy; therefore, they were much more likely than the girls to have had sexual intercourse in high school.

I don't mean to suggest that boys were unconcerned about getting a girl pregnant. Indeed, this is one reason why many refrained from sexual intercourse in those early years. But in most high schools, there were the "other" girls, the "sluts," the kind who, as several of the men said, "you screwed around with but wouldn't take on a date with your friends." Generally these were girls of lower status, largely because they also were lower-class. Metaphorically, then, they were the girls from what small-town America has always known as the other side of the tracks, the unknown, alien other who could be seduced without guilt, remorse or serious consequence—girls you could sleep with but would never marry. The girls from the "right side" were like one's sister, girls whose virginity a boy had a stake in, since one of them would most likely become his wife.

But things changed rapidly and the high school–college dividing line was soon to give way for both girls and boys. When those now in their late twenties and early thirties reached high school, somewhere between the late 1960s and the mid-1970s, college orientation already had little effect among boys and, while still retaining some influence among girls in the upper range of this group, continued to diminish with each succeeding cohort. By the time today's teenagers arrive on the scene, college orientation by itself has relatively little effect on the age at which first intercourse will occur. Undoubtedly, the increasing accessibility and acceptance of birth control,[4] the possibility of aborting an unwanted pregnancy[5] and the continuing liberalization of sexual norms, which has made premarital sex a common practice, all are important factors here. But it seems to me that the difference also is related to the fact that, compared with the older generations, many young people in the college-prep track today have no real reason to be there—no genuine commitment to learning or scholarship, no thoughtful plans for the future, whether in the work world or in their personal lives.[6]

For today's young, all the social structures that supported such commitments, that made planning for the future a reasonable enterprise, have been weakened substantially. Earlier generations of high-school students knew better what they were working toward. It made no difference whether they were working-class young who would go no further than high school, or the children of the middle class who knew they'd go on to college. Once schooling was finished, they could at least dream of finding good jobs and a stable family life in which they'd match, if not surpass, their parents' accomplishments.

For adolescents today, these are shattered dreams. The retrenchment and constriction of American industry make the job market highly uncertain, and inflation has turned what used to be a good wage into a bare living. Housing in most major cities of the country is so expensive that first-time homeowning is out of the range of any but the most affluent.[7] And complicating it all is the fact that gender roles, once so clearly defined, are in flux, with neither girls nor boys certain about what stable, committed family relationships might look like. Who works and how much, who bears responsibility for the care of children—these questions, once decided by fiat, all need to be discussed and negotiated now. It means wider options for both men and women, but it also makes life less certain in a time when insecurity is already very high. Consequently, while young people still have fantasies about love and romance, they have few illusions about marriage, family and lifelong stability.

Without the kind of stable structures—community, work, family—that are necessary to a belief in the future and a sense of progress, most teenagers find it hard to muster motivation for restraint of any kind. Yet there are many high-school students, male and female, who do have well-developed professional goals, and it is they who are most likely to delay entering the sexual arena. Perhaps because they're a little older, perhaps because their eyes are on the future, probably because of some combination of both, when they do become sexually active, they tend to choose their partners with care and to be consistent in their use of birth control. These are the youth who are least vulnerable to social trends and peer pressures, young people who are more inner-directed in contrast to the other-directedness of most teenagers.[8]

It's often not an easy path, however, especially for the boys, who are likely to come under fire from the rest of their classmates, to be derogated by both girls and boys with such labels as "nerd," "wimp" or "queer." Interestingly enough, there are no such disparaging words in general use for the virginal girl. When I asked about this, Carla, a 17-year-old high-school student from a small town in New Jersey, laughed and said, "God, I guess it isn't around enough to have a word for it." Then more thoughtfully, "I don't know, 'prude,' that's a word that's around, or 'goody-goody,' or just plain 'straight.' But nobody goes around bragging about it, and when people find out, they're surprised. It's like, 'Oh, she's a virgin? I can't believe it!' " All of which suggests perhaps that, while not necessarily an envied or emulated state, virginity still is not a stigmatized one.

For the women who came to puberty between the late sixties and the mid-seventies—those now in their mid-twenties to early thirties—the first intercourse was likely to take place sometime around their seventeenth year. For those who reached adolescence a decade later, women presently in their late teens and early twenties, not only was the age of first intercourse younger, but much of the angst and the concern about disgrace that characterized the decision making of the older women were gone. Instead, even teenagers spoke of feeling pressured because "the time had come" and said it was "a big relief" to have it done. Sometimes a relationship was involved. "It was a big relief actually," said 18-year-old Anne, a student at the University of Maryland, whose first time was at 15. "We had talked about it for a long time, and I told him I was afraid, so he didn't really pressure me. But I knew he wanted it, so finally I told him it was okay; I actually initiated it the first time. After all the talk, it was no big deal. I remember being distracted during the actual act and thinking: 'Gee, I'm finally losing my virginity.' "

For others, it was a fleeting encounter. "I was 17, right in the middle of my senior year in high school," recalled 20-year-old Beth, now a secretary in Chicago. "I met this guy in a café, and we hung around for a while and then wound up back in his apartment. I wasn't looking for someone to have sex with, but when the occasion came up, I thought: 'Oh good, it's time.' There was no physical or emotional satisfaction; it was your basic one-night-stand type of thing. But I enjoyed it because I thought: 'Oh my gosh, I'm having sex.' Afterwards it was different. I assumed there'd be some kind of a relationship. I didn't exactly feel sorry I did it because I was so glad to have it behind me. But I was real disappointed when I never saw him again."

Not infrequently, women of all ages spoke of "giving in" to the man in their lives because they felt it was the only way to hold him. Sometimes it was said blatantly. "I was afraid, but I loved him. I knew how badly he wanted to do it, and there are so many girls who'll do it with him, so I finally decided it was okay," said 14-year-old Marie from Cincinnati. At other times, it was a little more subtle. "It was right at the end of the tenth grade, just before my sixteenth birthday. My boyfriend was a senior, and he was going off to college and I wanted to cement the relationship before he left," said 22-year-old LuAnne, a Baltimore beautician.

Sometimes there was a real relationship to be protected or cemented. Often there was not, as the men involved knew all too well. "It was with a girl I had been going with in high school," said 25-year-old Rob, a Seattle graduate student. "I knew that she agreed to have sex with me because she wanted to solidify the relationship, but that's not where I was at all. She saw it as turning us into a solid couple, and I saw it as a coming of age and getting past something. It didn't have much to do with her or the relationship. I suppose even then I felt some guilt about using her like that, but, well, you know how it is."

Despite some revolutionary changes in sexual attitude and behavior, then, some things, unhappily, remain the same. For

girls, it's often still pressure from a boy she likes that's responsible for her initiation into sexual intercourse. Yes, she makes
the decision, as these stories tell over and over again. But for
too many it's a step taken in the context of her desire for the
relationship and her fear, not unfounded, that if she doesn't agree
he'll find someone who will.

Power! It's not a word we like to use when thinking about our
intimate relationships. Yet it's undeniable that in the relations
between the sexes the balance of power still falls heavily in favor
of men, largely because relationships and their management are
still uniquely the province of women. Why is it that way? Men,
after all, need relationships at least as much as women do.[9] Yet
it's women who assume the major responsibility for their care
and nurturance, women who are more likely to give up or give
in, to compromise some position, some part of self in the interest
of maintaining a relationship. What happens to our girl children
to make women so hungry for a relationship that they'll have
sex with a man to hold on to it?

The easy answer is their lifetime of training for compliance,
submission and attention to the needs of others—a process of
socialization in which all the institutions of society work quietly
but artfully to mold girls into proper women in accordance with
the accepted standards of the day. There's merit in the answer,
to be sure; these are powerful and effective forces in shaping
human life. But for these socialization processes to take root so
deeply, they must rest in soil that has already been tilled and
fertilized. To understand how this happens, we go back to infancy
once again.

The formation of a gender identity for a girl requires no breaks
with the past, as it does for a boy. She's a girl, mother's a woman;
the one, she understands intuitively, leads quite naturally to the
other. With no need to renounce her earliest identification with
a woman, she has no need to separate as completely and irre-
vocably as a boy must, or to build the kind of defenses against
feeling and attachment that he does. Therefore, instead of the
rigid boundaries a man develops as a means of protecting and
maintaining those defenses, she develops ego boundaries that

are more permeable, more easily breached—a fact of paramount importance in the management of both her internal life and her external one. For her sense of herself is never quite as separate as a man's. Rather, she experiences herself always as more continuous with another, and the maintenance of close personal connections will continue to be one of life's essential themes for her.

It's in this developmental scenario that we see the birth of women's concern for internal life and the world of relationships and of men's focus on external life and the world of achievement. His rigid boundaries serve to separate self from other, to circumscribe not only his relationships with others but his connection to his inner emotional life as well. Her more permeable ones keep her connected to others, making separation and the development of an autonomous, bounded self far more difficult.

This is the basic orientation we each bring to the world, an orientation that's not only nurtured but actively reinforced by our socialization to femininity and masculinity and the roles we each are expected to play—roles that define who we are, how we relate to each other, even how we experience life itself in pervasive and powerful ways. For women this means years of indoctrination to subordination, to putting self second to the needs and demands of others—training that takes so well because the soil has been seeded by the early childhood developments I have sketched here.

It's a neat fit, isn't it? A family structure that engenders deep-seated psychological differences between women and men, which then match so well with the social definitions of masculine and feminine. He grows up to attend to the large, impersonal issues of public life; she to concentrate on the smaller, personal ones of the private world. All of it getting its start in the social organization of the family.

Clearly the sexual and gender revolutions of recent decades have made serious dents in the old stereotypic definitions of femininity. Women are freer now than they have ever been to test themselves in a variety of ways of living, including the sexual. But the need for a relationship, for connection and attachment, continues to loom large in their internal life—a need that's women's strength in many ways, but one that also puts them at a distinct disadvantage in the battle between the sexes.

It isn't, I repeat, that men need relationships less than women. But a man can barricade himself behind his impenetrable boundaries, keeping his needs and feelings out of consciousness, hiding them not just from the world outside but from the one inside as well. A woman has no such easy retreat. His ability to distance himself from his inner emotional life means also that the split between sex and emotion is much easier for him than it is for her—a difference between them that puts a good deal of power on his side of the relationship. For she knows that it would, indeed, be relatively easy for him to find sexual satisfaction elsewhere. So she "gives in," forced not just by him but also by her own internal need to maintain the relationship *and* by her lifelong training to care for the needs of others.

The issue of power comes to the fore also in the histories of a small number of women (just over 5 percent) who as teenagers had their first sexual experience with an adult man, someone substantially older who held some position of power and authority in their lives—a teacher, a camp director, a psychologist, a father of a child for whom they babysat. "I was a senior in high school, and I made a conscious decision," recalled 32-year-old Laura, an Atlanta filmmaker. "It was a very difficult time in my life, and I was very depressed and very, very angry. I went to talk to my high-school counselor, who sent me to the school psychologist. I was very taken with him; I thought he was the most sensitive person I ever met in my life.

"One time when I was describing the tension and anxiety and all the feelings I was having, he asked me if it ever occurred to me that some of my feelings were sexual tension. Well, it hadn't, but right away I could see where he was going. I was enormously flattered and more than a little frightened. But he kept telling me how grown-up and sophisticated I was, so I kept trying to act that way. Eventually we became lovers, and I would say it was a pretty nice experience. I didn't have orgasms or anything, but I enjoyed sex."

"What was it that gave you pleasure?"

"Number one, I enjoyed the attention because I'd never had much of that; it made me feel special. I enjoyed knowing someone was so stimulated by me and that I was the only one in the high school having an affair with this special person who the other girls were dying over. And it gave me a sense of power to know I could inspire such feeling in someone else."

About half the women whose first time was with an older, high-status man said that, at the time, they thought it was exciting and wonderful. In retrospect, however, all voiced some doubts. "It seemed fabulous then, this attractive man who wanted me so much and who told me how beautiful and exciting I was," said 28-year-old Toby, a Denver paralegal, whose first time at 15 was with the father of the child for whom she babysat. "It wasn't tawdry, in the back seat of the car or anything like that, like some stories I've heard from other women. I was only a kid, but I felt like a very desirable woman who had this special secret love. It went on like that until I graduated high school."

"You said 'it seemed fabulous then.' Have you changed your mind about it now?"

"Well, yes, I guess so. I feel like I missed out on my adolescence. I mean, sure, there were some good things about it. It was a good way to get initiated into sex because he knew what he was doing. When I hear other women talk about how they got started, it's ugh, ugly. You know, two stupid kids groping around. It wasn't like that for me. I felt very cared for, and he taught me about my body and how to respond sexually. But I was so involved with him—emotionally, I mean—I didn't really date anyone in high school, so the rest of life wasn't much fun for me. And when I look back, I see how he used me. I was convinced I was making a grown-up decision. But how grown-up can a 15-year-old be, especially when this glamorous person is stacked up against some pimply-faced high-school boy? If I ever have a daughter, I'll do whatever's necessary—lock her in her room if I have to—to keep her from doing the same thing."

For the others who found themselves in the same situation, there was nothing at all wonderful about the experience. The

attraction, the excitement that accompanied the illicit, the thrill
of being desired by one who stood so tall in the world—all these
were there. But alongside them were the sense of danger, of
fear, and a quality of coercion that came close to rape. "My first
intercourse was shortly before I was 16, and it was scary," said
Nancy, a 31-year-old publicity agent from Augusta, Georgia, who
shuddered at the recollection. "He was the director of the camp
I went to and a coach at a high school in my town, and he was
married, too. He was this attractive, older man, and we were
in this teacher-student relationship, so I looked at him as being
worldly and knowledgeable and all that. I had a crush on him,
but I was pretty immature, and I wasn't ready for that kind of
a relationship. I mean, I liked his attention, and I wanted him
to love me. But I wanted to moon around about him; I wasn't
ready for sex. Then one day it just happened. He was all over
me before I knew it, and I felt completely out of control. I didn't
feel I had much choice. I didn't feel like I was raped exactly,
but I felt like I didn't have the choice to say no. It was awful.
It wasn't intensely painful or anything like that, just, I don't
know, awful."

None of these women claimed they were sexually abused.[10]
But they were sexual victims, nevertheless—victims of a powerful and predatory male who took advantage of their youthful
naïveté. For some, the experience was a good one while it lasted;
for others, it was not. But good or bad, it clearly was not without
cost, as is evident by their universal insistence that they would
move mountains to keep their own daughters safe from such a
liaison.

No matter what their motivation, no matter whether they
describe the experience as loving or painful, wonderful or terrible, the woman whose first time ended in orgasm was rare
indeed. For most women, including those who had masturbated
to orgasm for years before, an orgasm in the context of a sexual
interaction came much later. No surprise when women speak
so often about the discomfort or pain of that first time, and when
men say it was "too fast" for any real pleasure for either one of
them. "Besides being painful, the reason I thought it was so

miserable is because it was so male-oriented," complained a 36-year-old Seattle teacher, who was 19 when she first had intercourse. "I mean, it was directed to his coming, no sensuality, nothing soft and pleasurable. The so-called kid's sexual experiences I had before, with whatever guy I was with, were much more in the nature of mutual pleasuring. I used to think about those experiences and miss them and wonder why I ever got into doing the so-called real thing."

What I have been saying, then, is that while the act itself generally was disappointing, there were also gains for both women and men. Curiosity was abated, the mystery ended. For both, also, it was a step into the world of adult sexuality. But there the similarities end and the differences take over.

No woman talked about the first intercourse as defining of womanhood, a common theme for the men. Only one man said he had regrets and wished he had waited for a more appropriate person. But women of all ages frequently voiced regret—not because they were guilty, not because they were sorry to have done it, but because the romantic fantasy of the first time hadn't been fulfilled. "I just wish I had waited for a meaningful relationship. Then maybe it would have been more like I expected. As it is, I feel cheated," said a 30-year-old San Francisco florist, a note of sadness lingering in her voice.

Given the ambivalence with which women's sexuality continues to be held in our society, it's no surprise that women and men react so differently to something as significant as their first time. For despite the profound changes in sexual *behavior* which we have witnessed in these last decades, the old *ideology* and the feelings it wrought are not yet wholly gone from our consciousness. We need only look at the language we use about men, women and sex to understand the differences. Men score, they make it, they collect notches—language that connotes conquest and accomplishment. Women are seduced, they're taken, they give up their virginity—words that suggest submission and loss. He's the actor, she the acted-upon. He gains status; she loses it as she gives up this socially prized commodity. He's a stud; she's too easy, a slut. As 29-year-old Andy, a Memphis professor, put it so starkly: "It's different from what it used to be when women were supposed to hold out until they got married. There's pressure now on both men and women to lose their virginity. But for a man it's a sign of manhood, and for a woman there's still some loss of value. It's like two opposing traits, which puts us in opposite corners, like fighters in the ring."

Whatever the problems, the pain, the disillusionment of the first time, however, sex gets better with time and experience for most of us. But both the idea and the act will continue to arouse a complex set of emotional responses. They will be different from the feelings engendered by these early experiences, to be sure, but they will, nevertheless, be no less demanding of our attention and concern.

---

1. Cf. Lillian Breslow Rubin, *Worlds of Pain: Life in the Working-Class Family* (New York: Basic/Harper Torchbook, 1976). In this study, 80 percent of the young working-class couples had engaged in premarital intercourse and 44 percent married because the woman became pregnant.

2. John D'Emilio and Estelle B. Freedman, *Intimate Matters: A History of Sexuality in America* (New York: Harper & Row, 1988), Part IV; also Paula S. Fass, *The Damned and the Beautiful* (New York: Oxford University Press, 1977).

3. John Costello, *Virtue Under Fire* (Boston: Little, Brown, 1985).

4. It's true, of course, that the rate of teen pregnancy has exploded. But all statistics show that the live-birth rate is very different from the pregnancy rate. For example, in 1984, the birth rate per 1,000 for white teenagers 15–19 was 19.0, up from 10.9 in 1970. Among blacks of the same age, the live-birth rate was 87.1 per 1,000, down from 96.9 in 1970. Some of the pregnancies ended in miscarriage, but most of those that were terminated ended in abortion. Cheryl D. Hayes, ed., *Risking the Future*, Vol. I: *Adolescent Sexuality, Pregnancy, and Childbearing* (Washington, D.C.: National Academy Press, 1987), Table 2–16.

5. As I write, the U.S. Supreme Court has just returned to the states much of the power to control and regulate abortion that the 1973 *Roe* v. *Wade* decision took from them. With this latest move in the abortion struggle, the Court has added another dimension of uncertainty to the lives of the young, who, until now, have never lived in a time when abortion on demand was not legal.

6. It's true that in the past many women went to college to find a suitable

husband there. But this in itself was a serious objective, one the women did not take lightly, and one, also, that required them to delay becoming fully sexually active if they were to achieve their goal.

7. In San Francisco, for example, the median price of a house in 1989 was $268,000, an amount only 11 percent of the city's population could even contemplate.

8. For the origin of the terms "inner-directed" and "other-directed," see David Riesman et al., *The Lonely Crowd* (Garden City, N.Y.: Doubleday Anchor, 1956).

9. It's well established that men who are alone do much worse than women in many dimensions of living, whether physical or emotional. All the research available shows that married men live longer, healthier lives than those who are single. The reverse is true for women. Those who never marry live longer and with fewer physical and emotional problems than their married sisters. Losing a spouse may be difficult for both, but the life span of a woman is not affected by the death of her husband, even if she doesn't remarry. The same is not true for men, whose lives are in serious jeopardy if they don't marry again quickly. The reasons for these differences are complex. But, as I have argued elsewhere, they lie much more in the realm of the kind of emotional sustenance women provide for men than in the physical care they give. A man's dependent and relational needs, however, are rarely as obvious as a woman's because there's usually a woman quickly and easily available to help obscure them. Knud J. Helsing, Moyses Szklo and George W. Comstock, "Factors Associated with Mortality After Widowhood," *American Journal of Public Health* 71 (1981): 802–809; Lillian B. Rubin, *Intimate Strangers: Men and Women Together* (New York: Harper Perennial Library, 1984), Chapter 6; Mervyn Susser, "Widowhood: A Situational Life Stress or a Stressful Event?" *American Journal of Public Health* 71 (1981): 793–796. See also Jessie Bernard, *The Future of Marriage* (New York: Bantam Books, 1973).

10. Over 5 percent of the women I met had been victims of serious sexual abuse in childhood, usually perpetrated by a father or stepfather. I have not included these women in this chapter because the sexual and developmental issues raised by such early childhood experiences deserve treatment in their own right.

# 4

---

# *Teenage Sex*

*I*f there are two words that describe the sexual sensibility of today's youth, they are "tolerance" and "entitlement." *Nowhere are the effects of the sexual revolution more dramatically evident than in teenagers' sense of entitlement to make their own choices about sex and in their tolerance of all kinds of sexual behaviors, so long as they meet the current peer norms.* A sharp contrast to the young of earlier generations, among whom tolerance was limited and entitlement almost nonexistent.

It's the language of love and romance, not commitment and marriage, that defines the boundaries of sexuality for most teenagers today. No promises made, given or implied. "We love each other, so there's no reason why we shouldn't be making love," said 16-year-old Emily from Columbus, Ohio, her dark eyes fixing me with an intent gaze.

"Does that mean you've made a long-term commitment to each other?"

She hesitated and looked doubtful, then finally spoke: "I don't know what you mean by that. Do you mean are we going to get married? The answer is no. Or will we be together next year? I don't know about that; that's a long time from now. Most kids don't stay together such a long time. But we won't date anybody else as long as we're together. That's a commitment, isn't it? Just because we don't expect to get married doesn't mean we're not in love, does it?"

Data on teenage sexual activity are inexact, to say the least. But most experts in the field agree that somewhere over 60 percent of American teenagers have had sexual intercourse by the time they finish high school. A Harris poll in 1986 found that 57 percent of the nation's 17-year-olds, 46 percent of the 16-year-olds and 29 percent of the 15-year-olds had had sexual intercourse. In a finely tuned analysis of the national data, demographer Sandra Hofferth estimates conservatively that 66 percent are sexually experienced by the time they reach their nineteenth birthday.[1] Planned Parenthood puts the figure at 75 percent. And all agree that the age at which adolescents make their sexual debut continues to decline. A recent survey of eighth-grade students—that is, 14-year-olds—from three rural counties in Maryland revealed that 58 percent of the boys and 47 percent of the girls had experienced coitus.[2]

Even among teenagers brought up in conservative Christian families, the proportion who are sexually experienced is very high. In mid-1987, eight evangelical denominations in the central and southern states conducted a study of teen sexual behavior. The findings could have given little comfort to the advocates of sexual abstinence in the teenage world. Forty-three percent of the young people surveyed, all of whom attended church regularly, had had sexual intercourse before their eighteenth birthday, and an almost equal number had experimented with sexual behaviors short of actual coitus. Equally unsettling for their parents and ministers, well over one-third of these students refused to brand sex outside marriage as morally unacceptable.[3]

These impressive statistics speak to important changes in the culture of adolescent sexuality—changes that are especially profound for girls, since boys and men have always had more sexual leeway than girls and women. For boys, the big difference now is that, for the first time ever, their sexual exploration and activity need not be confined to "bad" girls only. No small change, it's true, but insignificant when compared with the shift for girls, who now have permission to be sexually active outside the context of love, marriage and commitment.

Still, there's something more to be said about the statistics we commonly cite about teenage sex. For while statistics may not lie, they often leave us with a distorted version of the truth. It isn't that the findings of the studies are wrong, but that, by the very nature of large-scale statistical surveys, they can get at only a small corner of reality. In the matter of adolescent sexual behavior, these studies ask such questions as: Have you ever had sexual intercourse? A yes puts the respondent into the sexually active category, a no into its opposite. But these are labels that tell us little about the reality of a young person's sexual experience, especially among the girls, even about whether they are sexually active or not.

Two-thirds of the teenagers I met had had sexual intercourse. Yet among those "sexually active" young people were several girls who, after trying it out once, decided to put the whole issue on hold. "It was with my boyfriend, who I'd been going out with for about seven or eight months," explained a 16-year-old Oakland girl, who looked around uncomfortably as she spoke. "We talked about it a lot, and we both decided we wanted to and, like, the time was right. It was the first time for both of us, and we decided we wanted to have sex for the first time with each other."

"And how did you feel about it afterwards?"

"It didn't affect me in the way I thought it would. I mean, I didn't sit around afterwards thinking: 'Gosh, I took this great, huge step.' I think I expected everything in the world to change, but the world just kept going on the next day just like it did the day before. But I do feel it was an important experience that maybe I should have done when I was older. I'm not sure. I don't have any regrets, but it wasn't exactly what I expected. I mean, it wasn't that bad, but it wasn't like it felt real good or anything. I'm glad the first time was with him, but I don't feel like rushing out and doing it again with him or anyone else, not in the near future anyway."

There are others who also would come up positive in the sexually active column yet who, on closer examination, turned out to have been abstinent for as long as a year or two at the time of our meeting. Seventeen-year-old Joanne, a high-school senior from Richmond, Virginia, had her first sexual experience about six months after her fourteenth birthday. "We had been together for four months, and he asked me to have sex. He didn't push me; he was very understanding. But we were really in love, and it felt like, why shouldn't we?"

"How was it for you?"

"It was fine. Everyone was saying, 'You'll be really scared the first time,' but I wasn't. I knew I really loved him a lot, and I knew he felt the same way about me. So it didn't bother me at all. I felt really close to him and I liked that, and I could tell he really felt close to me, too. It felt real nice. We went together for a year and a half, and since then I haven't had sex with anyone else."

"Do you want to?"

"No, not really, not now anyway. If I fall in love with someone, I'm sure I will—want to, I mean. But I haven't yet, and it's been over a year since we broke up."

Finally, there are those who had been quite sexually active, girls who at 14 or 15 had had more than one sexual experience, sometimes with several different partners, and in the process seemed to have scared themselves into celibacy. "I go to this Christian school, and a lot of the kids are into stuff they shouldn't be doing, you know, sex and drugs and things like that," said a 17-year-old New York suburbanite, the words rushing from her as if in a confessional. "It's not as bad as the public school in this town, but there's a lot of that stuff in my school, too. Anyway, I met this boy there who became my boyfriend for a little while. That was the first time I had sex.

"At the time, my parents and I weren't getting along, and I

was rebelling against them. So sex and drugs and all that was a good way to do it. But I always felt guilty and stuff; I'd wake up the next morning and feel miserable. Then the headmaster of the school found out about what the kids were doing, and they really cleaned house and expelled a whole bunch of kids. I was so terrified that they'd get me, too, but I was one of the lucky ones."

Interrupting the flow of words for a moment, she planted her elbows on the table, cupped her face in her hands and said quietly, "I was so relieved. I was getting more and more scared, like I didn't know what was happening to me, or why I was doing what I was doing. It seemed like I was trying to find a way to stop but didn't know how. I found out that sex without marriage is more physically enjoyable than it is mentally. So now I'm saving myself for when I get married. Maybe that's why I'm looking forward to marriage so much."

"What do you mean when you say sex was more physically than mentally enjoyable?"

"You know, it was nice; it feels good; it's nice to be close like that to someone you care about. But then you have all that guilt."

"Did you have orgasms?"

"Not at first, but after we were doing it for a while, I did— not all the time, but a lot of times."

Just as the words "sexually active" do not define the experience of such young people, so it is a travesty to describe most of the rest as "not sexually active" simply because they have not had sexual intercourse. Among the teenagers I met, just over one-third would fall into the "not sexually active" category of most large-scale surveys. Yet only seven had never engaged in any sexual play at all—all of them 13–15-year olds.[4]

Ironically, our historic and obsessive concern with virginity, which discourages sexual intercourse, unintentionally fosters behaviors no one thought to prohibit. Thus, most of those who had not yet had coitus engaged in all kinds of sexual practices, from genital fondling to mutual masturbation to oral sex. And the older they were, the more sophisticated the level of exploration and experimentation became. Indeed, by the time these "not sexually active" young people were finishing high school, fellatio and cunnilingus had become a significant part of sexual activity for close to half of them. "I don't mind giving a guy a blow job if he comes fast," said a Houston 17-year-old, fingering her long golden-highlighted brown hair as she spoke. "But with some guys it takes them a while to come, and my jaws lock, and that's not the most enjoyable thing in the world."

Anal sex, behavior that was almost unheard of among heterosexuals a couple of decades ago, also is part of the sexual discourse now, something kids talk about as a possibility, although only a few of them, whether they had had coitus or not, had tried it out before the end of high school. "I think whatever a couple does is their business; it's up to them," said 16-year-old Sara from Louisville. "There are things I won't do, like anal sex. My last boyfriend started to do it, and it hurt. It's terrible; I made him stop. But my best friend says she likes it, and if that's what she wants, that's okay. I don't think anyone has a right to judge what people do. It's nobody's business as long as the couple both agree."

Even the most conservative of the young people I met were firm in their belief that the choice about being sexual belongs to the individual alone. They make no judgments of others, and expect none to be made of them. "I have friends who are sexually active, and I think that's great for them," said 15-year-old Ying, a San Franciscan. "As far as I'm concerned, I think each person has to make their own decision about what they're going to do. If they're mature enough to handle it, that's fine; it's up to them. I can respect their decision, and I want people to respect mine. For me, I know I'm not ready, and I think it would be kind of dumb to do something I don't really want to do. But I don't know how I'll feel next year. If I meet somebody I really care about and it seems right, then I'd have sex."

"Do people respect your decision not to be sexual now?"

"Yeah, mostly. I mean, if you go to a dance or a party, there's always some boy who'll try. But I don't go to those things a lot.

And my real friends, they'd never pressure me about something like that. People mostly figure it's your business, and you'll do what you want."

The question of peer pressure is not quite so simple, of course. But generally it also is not the kind of direct, one-on-one pressure the adult world so often envisions. Instead, the pressure resides largely in the atmosphere itself—pressure that permeates all facets of teenage life, whether the style of dress, the language used, the music listened to or the initiation into sexual activity.[5] The need to belong, to feel one with the world in which we live, is common to all of us, adolescents and adults. Why else do fashions sweep the country, influencing not just the clothes we buy and the books we read, but personal habits of health and leisure? If everybody's wearing it, reading it, listening to it, doing it, the temptation to conform, to share in the experiences of those around us, is almost irresistible.

For adolescents who are struggling to separate from the family, to find a self-in-the-world that's uniquely theirs, a reference group against which to judge and measure themselves is a must. The peer group is the place where the possibilities of a self-yet-to-become can find expression. But like the family before it, this new group has its own needs for conformity among its members and its own requirements for acceptance. Paradoxically, then, the very group that facilitates the separation from the family and its restrictions becomes another arbiter of behavior in equally powerful ways.

When it comes to sex, it's not just the need to belong that exerts pressure, it's the need to know as well. A member of the peer group is the first to take the plunge and talk about it. It's news; it's consequential. For those who have not yet had the experience, it's riveting. Someone close has actually done it, can describe it, can say what it feels like. The veil of silence is pierced. But for the uninitiated, the mystery deepens; the pressure to know grows.

Undoubtedly there are instances when peer pressure is more direct and specific. The girl who is the first among her friends to have sexual intercourse may need to convince others to join her in order to assuage whatever guilt or anxiety may accompany her behavior. "I have to admit I was glad when a couple of my friends did it, too. It made me feel better that I wasn't the only one," said Lorie, now 18, as she recalled her feelings when she had her first experience at 15. "I didn't exactly try to talk them into it, but I didn't not try either. I mean, I talked about it a lot, and maybe I even made it better than I really thought it was so they'd get jealous and do it."

Some adolescents are able to resist all such persuasions. Most of these boys and girls stand outside the mainstream of peer culture and identify themselves—sometimes with pain, sometimes with pride—as "not in with the popular kids at school." A few, however, manage to withstand the pressure, whether around sex, drugs or alcohol, while still sustaining an identification with friends and peers whose behavior differs from their own. These generally are young people who exhibit a kind of personal magnetism that's unusual at any stage of life and who also have serious commitments to career or sports—a boy who's a committed runner and bicyclist, a girl who expects a college basketball scholarship, another who not only knows she's going on to college, but already has chosen a career path that requires an advanced degree. Their personal charm helps them to maintain status in the peer group, while their special interests enable them to keep enough distance to oppose its pressures.

Once in a while, there's someone for whom the example of friends and peers inspires restraint rather than the kind of titillation that seeks mimicry. "Whatever I do, I do in moderation; I know my limits," said 16-year-old Valerie, a Los Angeles girl, who spoke in a quiet, firm voice that matched the controlled, poised manner she exhibited throughout the interview. "A lot of people feel like when they get to high school, they have to become 'unvirgined.' I have no hang-ups about that. I'm not sexually active yet. I figure when the time comes, it comes, and I'll know it. I watch some of my friends and see the trouble they're getting into—you know, they get pregnant, or they're doing so bad in school that they'll never be able to get into a decent college. A couple of kids I know even dropped out of school. It's not at all appealing to me."

But these are the rare ones. For the rest, even though they may never have any conscious awareness of the pressure, it's clear that the peer culture in which they live and with which they identify is a powerful influence in their decision making about sex.

Boys have always felt the urgency to be one of the guys, whether in doing sex or talking about it. For them, the difference between the present and the past is only in the timing. The age at which they come under pressure to conform sexually is substantially younger today than it was a few decades ago. "I was 15 the first time I had sex, and before that I lied about it, told people I did it when I didn't," said a 17-year-old Chapel Hill boy, the discomfort on his face contradicting the words that seemed to come so easily.

"Why did you feel you had to lie?"

"There was always a lot of pressure from the other guys to join in the action, and I didn't want them to think I was a wimp or a nerd. You know, they were always talking about it, whether this girl or that one is a good lay, or about some girl who's got great tits, or somebody who likes it in the ass. And you want to be a part of it all, so you lie."

Girls, too, have always lied to accommodate peer norms. But in earlier generations, the sexually active girl played the role of the naïve innocent. Today the innocent pretends to be the sexual sophisticate. "I haven't found someone I feel comfortable with, so I haven't felt the need to have sex yet," said Hannah, a 15-year-old from suburban Chicago. "I don't see the point in rushing anything; I'm young; I have time. But only my very best friend knows the truth. The other kids don't know because I lie and say I'm doing things I'm not. As long as you say what they want to hear, nobody bothers you. It's when you're different that they don't like it."

According to the standards of today's adolescent culture, both boys and girls are expected to have sex with only one person at a time and to be true to the relationship. For most sexually active teenagers, therefore, serial monogamy is the rule. The definition of relationship, however, can be very loose. "A relationship is when two people decide they're going together, even if it's only for a weekend," explained 15-year-old Rick.

Most relationships probably last more than a weekend, but a month is a long time, and a year an eternity. To the adult mind, this seems shocking. But to the 15-year-old, for whom a year is such a significant proportion of conscious life, it is a very long time indeed.

Ideally, the norm calling for serial monogamy applies to all, regardless of gender. But, as is the case in any complex part of life, change and stability live alongside each other, sometimes easily, sometimes not. Therefore, there's a great distance between their ideal statements and the reality with which these young people live. In the real world, the double standard of sexuality that has for so long defined our sexual consciousness has been wounded, but is not yet dead. Consequently, a boy still has very wide latitude before he's criticized or censured, while a girl who is involved with more than one boy at a time will soon acquire a "bad rep." For her, the word is "slut"—a term in common use in high schools and colleges all across the land and one of unequivocal derogation. In a rather dramatic shift from the past, however, the girls are no longer so quick to be the enforcers of the sexual rules. In fact, they're far less likely to do the censuring now than they were in the fifties.

I don't mean to suggest that adolescent girls no longer render judgments on their peers or that a girl won't use the word "slut" to describe the behavior of another. But to the degree that they do, the standards by which those judgments are made are likely to be far more diverse than they were in the past and, more important, not so totally derived from the ideals of sexual conduct that, historically, have been decreed by those in power.

Obviously, no one is immune to the impact of those edicts. Adolescent girls, like their adult sisters and mothers, know quite well that men retain at least some of their ancient power to name women's behavior, to define what is worthy and acceptable and what is not. But most girls and women no longer accept such labeling without question or contention. This, in fact, is one of the unheralded gains of the feminist movement. The changes it has wrought in women's conception of self—in their belief in their right to define themselves and, at the very least, to participate in setting their own behavioral standards—have been so deeply internalized by now that they seem natural to the adolescents of this generation, as if it were ever thus. Consequently, teenage girls today not only are tolerant of an extraordinarily wide range of sexual behaviors, they also believe that, just as their own behavior is no one else's business, so it is with another's.

As with any of us, belief and behavior don't always match, of course. But many of the girls I met are conscious of the conflict between the two and persist in trying to reduce the dissonance. Even when they can't or don't, however, the girl who offends group norms usually isn't turned into a pariah and thrown into exile as she was in the fifties. "You know, it doesn't seem right that a girl gets a bad name; the guys sleep around all the time, and nobody calls them anything," said a 16-year-old small-town Texas girl angrily.

"Well, how do you feel about girls who sleep around?"

"I don't believe in it, and I don't really think anybody should do it. But, I don't know, I guess it's not my business, and I don't think it should be theirs either," she concluded emphatically.

For most men, however, the power to name and label is not given up lightly. Here again, I'm not suggesting that a man consciously sets out to control female sexual behavior or that any given man is aware that he's doing it. Rather, I'm saying that it's so deeply ingrained a part of the social fabric that it seems almost as natural as breathing. "A guy's got to know what he's getting into when he starts up with a girl," cautioned a 17-year-old Pittsburgh boy, straightening himself in his chair as if to make sure that his body language matched the certainty in his voice. "If you're looking for a girlfriend, not just some quick and dirty sex, you don't want to get involved with a slut, you know, one of those girls who goes out with more than one guy at a time, or a girl who goes for those one-nighters. You want her to be one of the nice girls, you know, the kind of girl who only has sex with her boyfriend, and she makes sure he's her boyfriend before she does it."

While male condemnation of girls who violate the norm of monogamy is ubiquitous, I never heard anyone speak about a boy with equal disparagement. Indeed, if they wanted to, they would have had a hard time finding a way to express their feelings, since there are no words in the lexicon of teenage life that would give evidence that any serious stigma attaches to a sexually promiscuous male. For him, the favored term is "stud," a word that traditionally has carried far more approbation than opprobrium. But here, too, there are subtle changes to suggest that girls are taking to themselves some of the power to name and label. Thus, when a girl uses the word "stud" now, it often is said sarcastically, carrying negative connotations and designed to warn other girls to beware. Among boys, however, the word still has the power to evoke images of masculinity and feelings of envy.

Certainly there are plenty of boys today who are sensitive to relationship issues, who say they only really enjoy sex when it's with someone they care about, who wouldn't be proud to be called a stud. But the same boys also find themselves envious of the guy who has such a reputation, even though his behavior may be distasteful to them. "There's these guys at school who are real studs, and sometimes I look at them and wonder: 'How do they do it?'" said a 16-year-old Cincinnati boy with reluctant admiration. "I don't know, I guess you can't help envying guys who can always get any girl. I mean, I don't like the idea of degrading girls or anything like that, but, well, I don't know, it seems like those guys are the ones who get the prettiest girls in school."

Change and stability, coexisting together, living side by side so peacefully that most of the time we don't even notice the contradictions involved. The changes in the world of adolescent sex, especially for girls, are massive and real: A teenage girl can now be fully sexually active without risk to her reputation and, therefore, to her sense of self. But some things remain doggedly, intransigently, the same: The power to determine the limits of her behavior, to legislate who's fit to be girlfriend, wife, mother, remains in the hands of men. Courts still declare a woman an "unfit" mother and take custody of her children from her because of her sexual behavior. Who ever heard of the phrase "unfit father"? And what is it that would make him "unfit"? Certainly not the fact that he's having a sexual relationship with a woman.[6]

Although most girls adhere to the norm of monogamy, however brief, a few refuse to be bound by the rules. Some of them were defiant when talking about their sexual behavior, using the language of liberation to justify what they do. "Why should the guys be able to do what they want and we can't? Dammit, I'm going to do what I want, and if they don't like it, screw them," insisted 16-year-old Betsy, who lives in suburban Washington and said she's had sexual intercourse, sometimes in a relationship, more often not, with "forty, maybe fifty different guys."

Sometimes these girls emulate traditional male behavior, bragging about their sexual exploits, counting each one as another scalp or notch for the scoreboard. "I've slept with eighty-five guys since I started two years ago, and I'm going for a hundred before school's out," said Debby, a 15-year-old from Cleveland.

Faced with such behavior, many boys respond with outrage. "Listen, it's not just guys who are out there these days. I know plenty of girls who collect guys like they're lipsticks or earrings, or some damn thing," stormed a 17-year-old boy from Baltimore, the words falling angrily from his lips. "You can find them at any party. All they want is to get their fuck; they don't give a damn about anything or anybody. If a guy wants to get close, even for a minute, it's 'Get lost.' "

"Do you get as angry at the boys who do that as at the girls?" I asked.

Looking surprised at the question, he thought for a moment, then replied, "Well, I don't think guys ought to do stuff like that either, but it's different, isn't it? Girls are always talking about feelings and stuff like that, but the ones I'm talking about, it's like they don't have any—anyway, not for the guys they sleep with, it seems like."

It's possible, of course, that there are girls who are as liberated as their words suggest, girls who have enough sense of self so that the degrading definitions with which they have been tagged create no emotional fallout. But I didn't meet them. Nor, if they exist, are they likely to be very large in number, since most people at any age aren't so self-defining and emotionally hardy that they can distance themselves so thoroughly from the evaluations of others in their environment. Indeed, few of us—man or woman, adolescent or adult—can ignore entirely the judgments of the larger society within which our lives are embedded.

It's true that girls like Betsy and Debby are likely to have a circle of friends within which their behavior is validated and supported sufficiently to satisfy the need to feel at one with others and to mitigate the sting of disapproval from the world outside. Still, it surely cannot be easy to expose themselves to the vulnerability that sex evokes knowing their partners are disrespectful and contemptuous. It's telling, in fact, that almost without exception these girls said they were not orgasmic in these fleeting sexual encounters. Partly this could be precisely because they were so quick, because the boys involved were not concerned with giving pleasure, only with getting it. But then, it seems to me reasonable to ask: What are the girls getting out of sex?

Yes, women often speak of pleasure in the experience even when there's no sexual gratification. But they usually mean that there's pleasure in feeling connected to another, that the closeness is affirming, that the sensual experience of being touched, held and hugged is important and satisfying, even when they don't come to orgasm. The kind of sexual encounters these girls describe, however—accounts in which the boys concur—seem to provide little enough of any of these.

Yet, some might argue, the very fact that so many girls feel free to experiment in this direction—that they choose this mode of making a statement about self and about their rights as females, that they use the language of liberation as justification—speaks powerfully to the changing definitions of female sexuality. There's undoubtedly truth in the argument. But, given the condemnation they still suffer, I believe also that, for a significant number of them, whether acknowledged or not, there's something more than sexual freedom that motivates their behavior, some other needs they're seeking to satisfy.

Some of the girls I met understood quite clearly that their sexual behavior was related to their relationships in the family, whether part of their rebellious struggle for independence or their pain and rage at what they perceive as parental neglect or indifference. "Since I was in the sixth grade, about 12, I guess, my parents have been fighting with me, telling me what to do. It's like all of a sudden I turned into some kind of a monster or something. Whatever I say, they don't believe me, so I figure if they don't trust me, why shouldn't I do what I want anyway?" complained a 16-year-old Boston girl, who became sexually active on her fourteenth birthday and claims over fifty partners. "It works out to about one every two weeks," she giggled. "God, they'd absolutely die if they knew"—a throwaway line that lets us know that, whatever else may be going on, at least part of her sexual conduct is designed to punish her parents.

Sometimes the parents of such girls really don't know. More often they do because their daughters find covert ways of getting the message to them. "I have sex with who I want, when I want, and nobody can stop me," said Melanie, a 17-year-old in Atlanta, whose defiant words sounded as if she were out to settle a score. And indeed she was, a reckoning with her father, who left the family without warning to live with another woman and her 6-year-old girl when his own daughter was 12. "It was like he traded me in for a younger model, just like he used to do with his cars," she remarked bitterly when she told the story of her parents' divorce.

"You sound as if sleeping with all these guys is paying your father back," I remarked.

"Yeah, well, he sure hates it. I mean, I don't exactly tell him up front, but it's no big secret. They both know, my parents, I mean, even though they pretend they don't. My father gave me this big lecture about love, and I told him I don't want to hear about any of that love stuff. It's garbage, just plain garbage. If a guy wants to make it with a girl, he'll say anything. I just spare them the trouble, that's all. Anyway, what's the big deal?"

With all her bravado, however, she needs the anesthesia of alcohol to pave the way. "I don't like drugs," she explained, "but booze, that's something else. You go to a party, get tanked, and then whatever happens, happens."

Over and over, girls talked about getting so drunk or stoned that they couldn't remember the next day what had gone on the night before. "I have to admit it; I'm usually so drunk at a party that I really don't know what I'm doing," said 16-year-old Jennifer, who lives in a Richmond suburb.

"Is that what makes it so easy for you to have sex with so many guys?" I asked her after she talked about how all she wanted was "a good, clean fuck."

"Yeah, I guess so. You know, you get to partying and having a good time, and pretty soon, anything goes. I see some dude who tempts me, and that's all there is."

Unfortunately, that's not "all there is." The Guttmacher Institute estimates that nationally 11 percent of unmarried teenage girls become pregnant each year.[7] This means that over 1 million American girls, one every ninety seconds, finds herself pregnant, a figure that's almost twice that of other Western countries, even though their rates of sexual activity and the age at which it begins match our own.[8] Not a surprise, then, that teenage girls account for just over one-fourth of the 1.6 million abortions performed in this country each year, or that 12 percent of the girls I met had experienced pregnancy, or that all but one of those ended in abortion.[9]

The reasons for our extraordinarily high unwed teen pregnancy rate are complicated enough to deserve a book of their own.[10] The subcultural variations of class, ethnicity and race all play a part. Poverty has its effect. Despair and hopelessness do not promote planning, whether long range or short.[11] Some teens get pregnant because, consciously or unconsciously, they want a child. It's their one chance to feel grown-up, to be taken seriously, to escape parental controls. For many, it's also the only thing they will ever have that they can call their own.

But for those in this study, this was not the case. Many of the girls I talked to, whether from middle-class or working-class families, had some college aspirations. Those who didn't dreamed more often of work and travel than of marriage and family. Even the one girl who didn't abort the pregnancy said she didn't think she was old enough to mother a child and gave the baby up for adoption.

Some experts insist that the problem lies in the family—a failure of both adult supervision and moral instruction. Undoubtedly there's some small truth in each of these. We know that parents' behavior is often in conflict with the words they speak, and that it's not unusual for the children of single parents to find some stranger in Mommy's or Daddy's bed. "She does it, so why can't I?" demanded 15-year-old Dana. And we know also that, with so many families in which both parents work at full-time jobs, there's always an empty house in the afternoon. But even when one parent doesn't work outside the home, even when the moral tone of the household is unequivocal in its opposition to premarital sex, it's not impossible to find a way. "My mother goes to Bible class two afternoons a week, and that's when we do it," said 17-year-old Robert in Richmond.

Sex educators argue that more and better knowledge about contraception is necessary to stem the tide of teen pregnancies. But it wasn't knowledge that was lacking for the girls and boys I spoke with, not even for those who had gotten pregnant.[12] These were sophisticated young people who knew the contraceptive score. Most had had sex education classes at school. Almost all said they knew about the various options, even though they might not use them. And few were unaware of the risks of either pregnancy or disease. Yet they took chances.

In 1976, I wrote that unmarried teenagers often became pregnant because planning for birth control implied preparation for the sex act, which was incompatible with their definition of self as a "good girl."[13] For them, unmarried sex was forgivable only if they were carried away on the tide of some great, uncontrollable emotion, feelings so powerful that nothing counted but the twosome. Certainly not cautionary tales, certainly not worries about pregnancy, or other mundane, worldly affairs.

Fifteen years later, there's still a great deal of social ambivalence, if not outright disapproval, about birth control for teenage girls. And those who plan for sex still face the prospect of being stigmatized by boys who reflect these attitudes. "You always know the bad girls; they're on the Pill," said George, an 18-year-old who lives in a small city near San Francisco. "It means they're always ready for sex; that's why they're taking it." An estimate that rubs off on girls and continues to make a very large proportion of them uncomfortable about contraceptive preparation. Indeed, so long as our society persists in making invidious distinctions between "good girls" and "bad girls" based on their sexual behavior and so long as the "good girl" is socially defined as one who is not self-consciously sexual, teenage girls will continue to play Russian roulette when it comes to birth control.

Alcohol, the most common drug in use in the high-school set today, provides one excuse to throw caution to the wind, one way of absenting the conscious self so that it cannot be held responsible for actions undertaken. With enough alcohol, inhibitions are put on hold, parental voices stilled, guilt and anxiety allayed. Conscience goes underground. "It's the liquor talking," adults say when they want to exempt someone from responsibility for word or deed. Why should it be different in the lives of our children? "I was so drunk I can't remember what I did last night or how I wound up in bed with three guys," a 16-year-old girl says, thereby implying that it wasn't something *she* did. It was the liquor talking! The responsibility for her untoward behavior falls to the effects of the alcohol. The self is in the clear, absolved of any wrongdoing.

Parenthetically, but surely not unimportantly, among the ordinary middle-class and working-class adolescents I met, more than one in ten showed clear evidence of alcohol abuse and an almost equal number were moving in that direction. Most were boys, but girls were not immune. And while the sale of alcoholic beverages to minors is illegal in every state in the nation, almost every teenager I spoke with agreed that "getting it is no problem." Once in a while the source was their parents' liquor stash. Much more often, there was no need to take such risks. "Where do we get the booze? No problem. Plenty of these small liquor stores around will sell to kids, especially once they get to know you," said 16-year-old Anthony in Denver. "And if one of them's not handy, all you have to do is stand outside any store and pretty soon somebody comes along who'll buy it for you. You give him the money, and he'll buy you whatever you want."

Since alcohol and other drugs are so much a part of teen life now, it's hard to know precisely how intimately they are entwined with sexual behavior, although the evidence of my research suggests that the relationship is close indeed. What we do know with absolute certainty, however, is that, drunk or sober, American teenagers are notoriously inconsistent about contraception. And the younger they are, the more likely they will be to slip, at least once in a while.

Sometimes the urgency of the moment comes together with the sense of invulnerability given to the young. "We didn't plan to have sex without a condom; it just happened," said 16-year-old Bonita from Louisville, as she explained how she got pregnant at 14. "We didn't always make love when we were together, and I guess he thought we wouldn't that day, so he didn't have anything with him. But then we began to make out and before you knew it, there we were."

"And you didn't think about the consequences?"

"I did, but . . . I mean, it's really hard to believe it can happen to you. I know that's stupid, but . . . well, it's true."

Sometimes, even when she's fully aware of the potential dangers, a girl doesn't feel able to insist that a boy use a condom. She may be too shy or insecure to assert herself in this way. "A few times he's wanted to do it without anything, and I always think, next time that happens I'll tell him he can't, but then I can't make the words come out of my mouth," sighed Genevieve, a 15-year-old from Trenton, New Jersey.

Sometimes she may be reluctant to damage the romance of

the moment. "It's hard to stop everything and make your boy-friend put on a rubber," said a 17-year-old New Yorker. "It makes everything seem so . . . so . . . I don't know, unspontaneous."

Sometimes she knows how much her boyfriend hates to wear the condom, so in a loving moment she gives him a gift. "I know how happy it makes him when he doesn't have to wear that thing, so sometimes I let him," explained Mariel, a 15-year-old from Indianapolis.

All of which brings us to the subject of AIDS. I asked everyone in this study, adolescent and adult, if they worried about the disease. Some people, more often adolescents than adults, said they were unconcerned. "Why would I worry about it? I don't sleep with gay guys, and I don't hang out with people who shoot dope," said a 16-year-old from Connecticut airily.

"How can you know what some of the people you've been involved with did in the past or might be experimenting with now?"

"Oh my God," she said, shaking her head as if mystified by my ignorance, "I go to school with these guys. Everybody knows what people are doing; you don't keep things like that secret. Anyway, what's the big deal? Show me one kid like me who's got AIDS."

Most young people, however, did say that AIDS worried them. But as is the case with any issue in American life, whether health or politics, attitudes don't necessarily get translated into behavior. In fact, more often than not there's a wide gap between the two—a split that's particularly sharp on the issue of AIDS.

Just as the adolescent sense of immortality and invulnerability influences contraception decisions, it tends to dominate their behavior about AIDS as well. Studies around the country con-firm my findings: Most teenagers don't use condoms and even those who say they do aren't necessarily consistent about it.

When I asked whether they would talk to a potential partner about AIDS or any of the other sexually transmitted diseases before agreeing to have sexual intercourse, most brushed off the question as wholly irrelevant. "Hell no, I wouldn't do that!" exclaimed Kevin, an 18-year-old from Atlanta, who looked at me as if I had just flown in from the moon. "I don't go picking up strange girls in a bar or something like that, so why would I worry?"

"But surely you know that that's not the only thing to worry about. Anyone you know could have been infected at some time in the past."

With a wave of his hand, "Yeah, yeah, I know all about it. But I don't know anyone with AIDS. I've never heard about even one straight person getting it unless they're junkies, and I don't go with people like that. So what's there to worry about?"

Pregnancy, AIDS, herpes, chlamydia, genital warts, gonorrhea, cytomegalovirus and a half dozen other sexually transmitted diseases most people still haven't heard of—all clear and present dangers, all affecting the young of all classes, cultures and races. Good reasons for parents to be troubled by the sexual behavior of their adolescent children. Ironically, many of these parents were themselves the children of the sixties, the same women and men who helped to hoist the flag of the sexual revolution of their own youth. Yet now they look with distress at their own children, who, it would seem, are simply finishing what they started. "It's all these diseases that are around now," they say. "Because having sex can kill you now," they insist.

Perhaps it's true that some parents wouldn't be concerned about the sexual conduct of their children if it weren't for the diseases that abound now. As the generation that claims the sexual revolution as its own, they generally have much more open attitudes about sexuality than those that dominated their own early lives. In the course of another research project, in which I was studying families with teenage children, most of the parents I met said they didn't expect their daughters to be virgins when they married, and they insisted they were perfectly comfortable with the idea. They talked about having brought their children up to be at ease with their sexuality, to be able to act on it responsibly at some appropriate time. What they didn't count on was that the children would redefine the "appropriate time," that the age at which they would enter into sexual activity would drop so precipitously. "We've always had a very open household about sex and my kids were raised to be comfortable with their sexuality," explained a 45-year-old New York mother of two teenagers. "I just assumed that when they got to be young adults—you know, 18 or 19—they'd be having sex. I don't think it ever occurred to me they'd be starting when they were still practically babies."

As they confronted these new realities, all the parents in that study, those who called themselves sexual liberals as well as those who were avowedly conservative, expressed grave misgivings about their children's sexuality that went well beyond concerns about disease, pregnancy or any other aspect of their physical welfare. "They're so young," they said. "What's their hurry?" they asked. Even parents who had been in the vanguard of the sexual revolution of the sixties found themselves in conflict, wanting to remain true to their beliefs, but anxious and fearful about what their children are doing now. "It was different," said a Berkeley mother of a sexually active 15-year-old boy as she recounted her own unorthodox sexual history. "I was in college, not in junior high or high school. Now it's too young; they don't know what they're doing yet."

"It's complicated; I have mixed feelings about it," said a Phoenix father of a 14-year-old son and a 16-year-old daughter, who described his earlier years as "sexually very experimental." "Do I have different feelings or wishes for my son and my daughter? Intellectually, no; actually, yes. I don't want her to get in too deep too fast. It's not that I'm against her having sex, but how can you be sure she's dealing with it wisely? Sure, I wish for a world where sex was less loaded and could be freer; my generation tried to make one. But I know it doesn't exist. And I have a particular concern about how sexuality is loaded for girls, so I guess I have to admit I think she's too young and I wish she'd wait. Not that that'll make any difference, you understand," he concluded with a shrug and a troubled smile.

How can we understand such parents? One popular explanation is that they have been co-opted into the life of mainstream America and abandoned the principles for which they once fought. But I believe there is another more complex

way to account for the fears and feelings they now express—
an explanation that addresses the lifelong issues of identity
formation.

We know, of course, that there are shifts and changes in
identity as we take on new roles and adapt to different life stages.
Each passage—from single to married to parenthood, for example, or from youth to mid-life to old age—calls upon a heretofore unrealized part of the self which, when consolidated and
internalized, leaves us with a new and different sense of who
we are. But each new definition of self doesn't wipe out the last
one. Rather, it is layered over all that came before, each suc-
cessive self-image becoming part of the complex and often conflicting patchwork that defines the self. Thus, the radical or
deviant identity we adopt in our youth remains with us, part of
the experience and definition of self, even when we no longer
act on the values it embodied, sometimes even when we no
longer believe in them.

It's a common experience for people in all generations. The
woman who defined herself as a flapper at 20, for example, still
thinks of herself that way 60 years later when she's 80, even
though no remnant remains of her old bohemian way of life. The
impoverished radical, the outsider of the thirties, may live the
life of a wealthy professional in the nineties. But he still sees
himself as marginal, a man who stands outside acceptable society, forever the radical outsider. The hippie of the sixties long
ago traded the commune for a house in the suburbs, while retaining a connection to the earlier unconventional self.

So it is with many of the sexual revolutionaries of the sixties.
Listening to them is often like hearing two different people, for
they have carried the old identity into adulthood alongside the
newer, more conventional one. The youthful deviant speaks ar-
ticulately about the value of sexual freedom and experimentation;
the mature adult speaks with the voice of the parent whose
deepest wish is to protect the children from possible harm.
Abstractly, they don't oppose teenage sex, but they worry that
they're "too young," that they won't "deal with it wisely."

No matter what the sexual experiences of their own past,

parents, teenagers and sex generally make an uneasy mix at best. The findings of a 1988 Gallup poll asking teenagers what topics they would most like to be able to discuss with their parents provide little comfort. Sex tied with religion for the bottom of the list. Forty-three percent of the adolescents polled said they'd like to talk more about family finances; only 28 percent wanted more discussion about sex.

These results will come as no surprise to most parents who have tried to talk about sex with their adolescent children. They have experienced firsthand the way the whole body tenses—the wary eyes suddenly refusing to make contact, the face held stiffly immobile so as to betray no emotion, the expressionless voice responding in monosyllables only. In fact, even when their own anxieties and ambivalence make them question their sexual behavior, most teenagers are afraid to risk talking to their parents about sex.

Partly that's because they don't trust that they will be heard and understood, that parents will be able to step out of their own shoes and into theirs before making judgments or giving advice. Partly it's because young people often feel that their parents are intrusive, that they leave them little room for private thought, let alone for private behavior. Sex is the one thing adolescents feel fully justified in keeping to themselves. The ethos of privacy and silence about our personal sexual experiences makes it easy to rationalize the refusal to speak. But their resistance is rooted in the adolescent struggle to separate from the family, in the search for autonomy, for an identity and a set of values they can call their own.

Not surprisingly, it isn't only parents whose intrusions are in the interest of restraining sexual behavior who come under fire. Those who want to live vicariously through their children, who give implicit encouragement to the children to act out the parents' own unmet fantasies, are equally suspect. "My mom's always coming into my room and wanting to talk, not just about sex, about everything," complained 16-year-old Tracy, a Chicago girl, who was a virgin when we met. "I love her and everything, but I wish she'd stay out. *It's my life, not hers. I don't want to have to tell her everything; it's not her business.* Some things are private, and sex is one of them. I'll do it when I'm ready, and I don't need her in the rooting section."

Most people today understand that the insistence on celibacy before marriage is little more than a nostalgic dream. But questions remain: At what age is the full expression of sexuality developmentally appropriate? What is too young today? "You may see the body of a woman on the outside, but the internal development of a 14-year-old is that of a child," replied a San Francisco developmental psychologist who is also the mother of a 15-year-old daughter. "Kids that young just aren't ready for sex and all the emotional stuff it generates. And they're not ready to be responsible either. Look at all the teen pregnancies."

But most theories of adolescent development were conceived decades ago, when the culture of teenage life was very different from the one our children live in today. What does it mean to an adolescent girl or boy to live in a peer society where being sexual is a taken-for-granted right? Does it make sense to assume that their response to their sexuality is no different than ours was in some earlier time?

Equally important, all developmental theories are built on the experience of the average individual, which means that any theoretical answer will assume more maturity in some people and less in others. But individual development can be stubbornly capricious, pushing at the limits of theory, challenging its most cherished postulates. The blanket answers such theories offer, therefore, are of relatively little use in figuring out where on the developmental continuum any particular child will fit.

Most experts agree that a woman's ability to be orgasmic is related to her comfort about her sexuality. If 15 is too young, what do we make of the fact that about a third of the 15-year-old girls who were having sex in a caring relationship reported that they had orgasms most of the time? What do we make of the story, told by a man now in his mid-30s, about his first sexual experience at 15? "You know how other kids think their parents are terrible. I was just the opposite. I couldn't figure out how these two wonderful people could have had me for a kid. I felt totally worthless, and I wanted to die. Then I fell in love with this girl in my class—whatever that means at 15. It saved my life. Being with her, making love with her, made an enormous difference in how I felt about myself. I began to feel like if she could love me, maybe I wasn't so bad. The year we went together was the only happy year of my life until then. Sure, the relationship was terribly incomplete, but that doesn't mean it didn't have some very deep meaning for us.

"We weren't just having sex either," he added, with a smile of recollection. "In fact, it's amazing, we didn't know what the hell we were doing; we were two dumb kids tumbling around on this uncomfortable couch. I didn't know anything about the clitoris or oral sex or anything else for that matter. But we were really making love. We would lie on that couch touching each other and exploring each other's bodies for hours and hours. In the intervening years, I've learned a whole set of tricks and how to use them, and now it's all over in fifteen to twenty minutes."

It's true, of course, that we don't know what the future holds for today's 15-year-olds, how they'll interpret their teenage experiences ten or twenty years from now. But at least in the present, I have heard others, both girls and boys, speak equally eloquently about the healing and restorative powers of a loving adolescent relationship.

These caveats notwithstanding, there's cause for concern as we watch our children move toward sexual exploration at younger and younger ages. As we seek to understand something of what motivates them, we would do well to look at the larger forces in the society, at the ways in which so much of everyday life has been sexualized, at how much sex—not the beauty of Eros and intimacy, but a tawdry, exploitative focus on sex as an object, a commodity for sale—has penetrated our consciousness and permeated our lives.

We would do well, also, to listen to our children, who often understand more than we think. "One reason kids have sex when they do is because after you've done it, you feel a lot more grown-up," said 16-year-old Allison of Richmond.

"Could you explain to me what it means to you to be grown-up, why it's so important?" I asked.

The words rushed from her as if the thoughts had been clamoring to be spoken. "You want to be grown-up because as a teen you don't count. When you're an adult, you get to be an active part of the society. You're someone who counts, not someone who's set off in their own teen world. You have a real status in the society; you're not just someone who's a problem. People listen to you; they care what you think. As a teenager, who cares what you think?"

It's an illusion of adulthood these young people gain, of course. But it does tell us something about why they seem to be in such a rush to get there. For the real issue is that adolescents today have no real function in our society, no reason for being except as a way station on the road to adulthood. And it explains also why several of the young people I met—both from the affluent middle class and from the struggling working class—put boredom and an absence of responsibility high on the list of explanations for behavior ranging from sex to drugs. Even those who work spoke of having nothing of consequence to do, since work generally is of little interest, dull jobs held only to earn enough money to buy the material accouterments of teenage life that seem so necessary to them.

*Boredom and the absence of responsibility*—complaints from a generation of children who have suffered all the contradictions of the quixotic child-rearing patterns of our age. On the one hand, from early childhood on, they have been encouraged to independent thought and action, their opinions solicited, often deferred to. On the other, they have been protected from responsibility by parents who believed they were entitled to a childhood free from care. Now, at adolescence, they insist on their right to fully autonomous status, but once they get it, they have little or nothing to do with it. "We're all bored, that's why we drink and do all that other stuff," said Derek, a 17-year-old from Augusta. "I think adults make a big mistake when they don't make sure kids have real responsibilities. I don't mean like cleaning our rooms and stuff like that, I mean *real* responsibilities and things we have to do, just like they have."

It's too simple to place the blame on parents alone, however. Yes, they must take some responsibility for having raised children who are bored and irresponsible. But it's hard to do otherwise in a society where adolescents have no role or function, where the word "community" no longer has much meaning, where politics fails to inspire commitment to the large social issues of the day, where the continuing rape of the environment leaves us fearful and uncertain about a future, where those in public life seem to value self-aggrandizement and the accumulation of wealth above all else, where the focus on self and personal gratification has taken on the quality of a new religion. This is the malaise that underlies our children's complaints about boredom and the absence of responsibility. And these are the long-term issues we must conjure with if we hope to see the generations yet to come abandon the kind of sensation seeking that's so common today.

———————•———————

1. "Influences on Early Sexual and Fertility Behavior," in Sandra L. Hofferth and Cheryl D. Hayes, eds., *Risking the Future*, Vol. II: *Adolescent Sexuality, Pregnancy and Childrearing* (Washington, D.C.: National Academy Press, 1987), p. 8.
2. Cheryl S. Alexander et al., "Early Sexual Activity Among Adolescents in Small Towns and Rural Areas," *Family Planning Perspectives* 21, 6 (November/December 1989): 261–266. See also Sandra L. Hofferth, Joan R. Kahn and Wendy Baldwin, "Premarital Sexual Activity Among U.S. Teenage Women over the Past Three Decades," *Family Planning Perspectives* 19 (1987): 46–53.
3. Reported in the San Francisco *Chronicle*, February 2, 1988.
4. Five of the seven were from immigrant Asian families, whose adolescent children, even when they chafe at the tight parental reins, don't often violate the rules.
5. In her history of the youth of the 1920s, Paula Fass examines in detail the way the peer group gains conformity to sexual norms by encouraging and including those whose behavior conforms to accepted standards and pun-

ishing and excluding those whose behavior does not. *The Damned and the Beautiful* (New York: Oxford University Press, 1977).

6. In this era when child sexual abuse has been such an agonizing issue in our society, an accused father may be judged unfit. But even here, courts around the country are loath to believe the worst and often refuse to strip divorced fathers of unsupervised visitation rights, sometimes in the face of substantial evidence of sexual violation of their daughters.

7. Personal communication, March 16, 1989.

8. The difference in teen pregnancy rates is most striking among those under 15. Moreover, American teenagers are five times as likely to give birth as girls in any other developed country in the world, a striking difference which reflects our social ambivalence about both contraception and abortion. See Cheryl D. Hayes, ed., *Risking the Future*, Vol. I: *Adolescent Sexuality, Pregnancy, and Childbearing* (Washington, D.C.: National Academy Press, 1987); Hofferth and Hayes, eds., *Risking the Future*, Vol. II; Elise F. Jones et al., *Teenage Pregnancy in Industrialized Countries* (New Haven: Yale University Press, 1986).

9. In an article entitled "Teen Pregnancy and Its Resolution," in Hofferth and Hayes, eds., *Risking the Future*, Vol. II, Hofferth cautions that without a national requirement for reporting abortions their number may be underrepresented by as much as 50 percent. Nevertheless, the available data show that about 40 percent of teenage pregnancies have been terminated by abortion each year since 1980.

10. See Kristin Luker, *Taking Chances: Abortion and the Decision Not to Contracept* (Berkeley: University of California Press, 1975).

11. Women with incomes below $11,000 are 15 percent of the population and 33 percent of all abortion patients. Women with incomes between $11,000 and $24,999 are 29 percent of the population and 34 percent of all abortion patients. Thus low-income women are about three times more likely to have an unwanted pregnancy than those who are more affluent. *National Abortion Federation, Statistical Abstract, 1988.*

12. A recent review of five studies that examined the effect of sex-education programs in the schools concluded that such programs have little or no effect on changing sexual behavior, whether in influencing decisions about sexual activity or in promoting the use of birth control. James W. Stout and Frederick T. Rivara, "Schools and Sex Education: Does It Work?" *Pediatrics* 83, 3 (March 1989): 375–379.

13. Lillian Breslow Rubin, *Worlds of Pain: Life in the Working-Class Family* (New York: Basic/Harper Torchbook, 1976), p. 63.

# 5

## The Transition Generation

"Make Love, Not War"—the slogan of the sexual revolution of the sixties. "Sex was a political statement then," said 40-year-old Larry, a Philadelphia architect, who leaned forward intently to give emphasis to his words. "There were no singles bars or anything like that. It was a different time; it wasn't just sport fucking. You went to demonstrations and peace marches, that's where you met people. It's hard to describe what it felt like. The closest thing to it, I guess, would be like life during wartime. Life became important to think about, not just to take it for granted. We were all in it together, and making love proved you weren't part of the madness. You cared about the people you were sleeping with, even if you just met them, because people who were out there on the streets together *felt* like they knew each other."

This was the era of mass political action, of civil rights protests and antiwar demonstrations, of peace marches and civil disobedience—street politics that became theater of the streets. University campuses were turned into battlegrounds, as students challenged everything from campus rules and requirements to the war in Vietnam. Confrontations with the police were a regular occurrence. Film clips of students being dragged off by the hair or beaten with a billy club were part of the nightly television news. Thousands who never dreamed they'd see the inside of a jail cell found out firsthand what it was like.

Among those who were active in the social and political struggles of the day, a kinship evolved, born of the sense that they were part of something larger than self; that, as Larry said, they "were all in it together." As Todd Gitlin, sociologist and chronicler of the sixties, has written: "The [New Left] movement, along with the rampant counterculture, was a sexy place to mix. Common bonds could be presupposed; strangers were automatically brothers and sisters. Meetings were sites for eyeplay and byplay and bedplay."[1]

This sense of unity bound people together and, more often than not, imbued their sexual encounters with meaning beyond simple need or desire. Two people came together exhilarated by the shared struggle, wanting to savor the events of the day, to preserve the excitement, to bring joy and comfort, to touch each other in yet a deeper way.

This was the backdrop against which the early days of the sexual revolution were played out—young people in revolt, not just against a war but against a whole set of values and institutions that supported American life at the time. The constraints against sexual expression were just one among the many targets of the day. Intellectuals who argued that sexual repression was the basis on which other forces of oppression took root became the gurus of revolutionaries on campuses around the country.[2] It was a revolution of hope, a celebration of change. Limits were pushed, rules challenged, boundaries violated. Sex was enveloped in an atmosphere of excitement and discovery. Ideologically, at least, the words "making love" still had some meaning. Not necessarily the romantic love with which sex had been associated for so long, but love that flowed from comradeship and that was expressed with some degree of mutual caring and concern.

It wasn't long, however, before idealism turned to exploitation and the phrase "making love" became little more than a euphemism for having sex—a failure of ideals not given to this revolution alone. For it is one of the tragic contradictions of so many revolutionary movements that the ideology continues to speak the language of freedom while the lived reality becomes yet another repressive force. Commenting on just such a shift in the sexual ethics and behavior of the men in the New Left, Gitlin wrote: "As the movement heated up, its celebrities notched more conquests. The smoldering mixture of danger and notoriety seemed to make men more predatory. The style of long-drawn-out heartfelt triangles yielded to furtive hit-and-run. . . . In the rush toward the phantasmagorical revolution, women became not simply a medium of exchange, consolidating the male bond, but rewards for male prowess and balm for male insecurity."[3]

"Girls say yes to guys who say no" became a recruiting slogan of the antiwar movement. The promise of a woman's body in exchange for a heroic stand, an inducement as old as time. The difference was only that in earlier eras it was the soldier who won a woman's favor; during the Vietnam War, it was the man who refused to serve. "God, when I think how naïve we were!" said Marianne, a 39-year-old Atlanta office manager, anger and disgust flitting across her face as she spoke. "There was a hell of a lot of abuse and manipulation in those relationships, a hell of a lot, and a lot of women look back and see how they were used in the name of sexual freedom."

By the late sixties, some of the women who had pioneered the sexual revolution began to take stock of their relationships with men, sexual and otherwise, and decided they didn't like what they saw.[4] As a result, they raised their own call to action and another revolutionary movement, Women's Liberation, was born—this one dedicated to sweeping changes in gender roles and relationships in both public and private life. In Consciousness Raising groups across the land, women talked about men and sex, compared notes, asked questions, analyzed their behavior. For these women, the wide-eyed aura of love and discovery that fueled the early days of the sexual revolution was replaced by power struggles as old as the relations between the sexes. While one war raged in the jungles of Vietnam, another began right here at home, in the kitchen, in the living room and, not least, in the bedroom. In the words of the day, the personal had become political.

A few of these women forswore men. Most continued to relate to them, but began to assert their sexual needs more forcefully and to demand greater sensitivity from the men in their lives, whether in a casual encounter or in a relationship. "The word was, if you want to fuck somebody, do it," recalled 42-year-old Anne, a Boston physician, whose blue eyes filled with wonder and amusement as she described the ethos of the times. "But it became a political thing. If he wanted to have sex with you, a guy would have to do it your way, not his. Silly things sometimes, like insisting you had to be on top, even if you didn't *really* want to. It was a funny time; there was this odd combination of being very angry at men and also being very much involved with them."

For the men who were relating to these women, the new demands, both in bed and out of it, the sudden onslaught of criticism of behaviors that until then had seemed acceptable, left them feeling misunderstood, bewildered and besieged. "It was really a crazy time," recalled a 42-year-old Milwaukee executive, his tone still sounding the bewilderment he felt then. "There was all this fucking around together, more than ever before, but we couldn't talk to each other. I felt like I was being bombarded with criticism all the time, and like I had to apologize for being dumb enough to be born male and doing male things, not just in bed but everywhere."

While some women made their voices heard and some men listened, for most people the sexual revolution rolled along without much change. As is so often true in periods of rapid social change, the language may have been different, but the sexual relationships remained much the same. "It seemed like overnight it went from 'I really love you, baby, so why can't we?' to 'If you're sexually free, you'll sleep with me.' Same guy; new line," said 40-year-old Marcia, a Berkeley pharmacist.

This is not to deny the very real gains for women in the sexual revolution. For the first time in our history, women were not just permitted but exhorted to experience the full force of their sexuality, to take pleasure in its expression, to celebrate it publicly rather than to conceal it as some private shame. "It was a wonderful time in many ways. Sexually I felt free and powerful and like I was in control," said Linda, a 41-year-old saleswoman, whose smile lit her face. Then, more soberly, "I was lucky, I guess, because I didn't get into some of the bad scenes that were around then."

It wasn't women alone who were the beneficiaries of these changes. For men, too, something new and profoundly important had taken place. True, men had always had access to sex without marriage. But always before it was a furtive affair in which they either had to seduce a "good" woman—a seduction whose outcome sometimes forced them into a marriage they wouldn't have chosen freely—or had to settle for unsatisfying sexual release with a prostitute or other "bad" woman. For the first time, there was the possibility for sex among equals, sex with a "good" woman who made a free choice, a woman who was neither guilt-ridden nor shamed by the expression of her sexuality, a sexual connection that was also a freely given emotional exchange.

That was the ideal. In some ways it worked for the men. "It was great, just great," exulted Bruce, a 45-year-old telephone installer from Tacoma. "It seemed like all of a sudden everybody felt freed to explore themselves and each other, and we could pack in all the old games and lines. What a relief!"

But for the women, ideology and reality were soon in conflict, and sexual liberation lived side by side with coercion and exploitation. The revolution, which had freed them to say yes, also disabled them from saying no. "It was weird; it was so hard to say no," said 38-year-old Paula, a furniture designer in Pittsburgh, whose brow wrinkled in puzzlement as she recalled those years. "The guys just took it for granted that you'd go to bed with them, and you felt like you had to explain it if you didn't

want to. Then if you tried, you couldn't think of a good reason
why not to, so you did it."

This was the bind women found themselves in, one of the
several paradoxes in which the sexual revolution was caught: For
the first time ever, American women were free to feel the power
of their sexuality and to act on it according to their desires. At
the same time, a lifetime of training to put the needs of others
before those of self made it difficult suddenly to make decisions
in their own behalf. Even when they were ready to do so, most
women had so little experience in attending to their own sexual
needs and desires that they weren't always sure what they might
be. "Everything changed so suddenly; it wasn't always easy to
know what your own sexual feelings were. Were you doing it
because it was the thing to do or to please some guy or what?"
explained 42-year-old Nancy, a Santa Barbara lawyer. "It wasn't
just that you were supposed to lose your virginity—*that* was no
big deal—but then you had to be sexually free. Who knew what
that meant? There was no context for this freedom; there were
no models and no guidance about how it could be. So we had
all this freedom and didn't know how to live with it. And there
were all these guys—just think what they were looking at; it was
like a dream come true for them. All these women who suddenly
weren't supposed to say no anymore. Well, the men didn't know
what to do with it either, so it became a new version of the old
male-female game.

"My struggle—and I guess it was true for a lot of other women,
too—was over having enough faith in myself as a person so I
could really know what I wanted to do and resist the pressure
from the guys. I got quite heavy for a while during that time; it
was the first and only time in my life I was ever overweight.
And I think it was a way of protecting myself, like I was saying,
'I'll show you; I won't be attractive, then I won't have to deal
with all this.' "

How could it have been otherwise?

Generations of women had been brought up to believe that
virginity was their most precious possession, their passport to
upward mobility, therefore to be guarded tenaciously until the

"right" moment. Generations of men had internalized conceptions of good women and bad women, had thrilled to the idea
of the chase and the conquest. Men could; women couldn't. Men
persisted; women resisted. These were the rules. Even where
premarital chastity was the ideal for both, male sexuality was
understood to be too unruly to be fully contained and transgres-
sions were forgiven. Not so for women, who were cast out of
respectable society, doomed to be scorned as "fallen women."
The language itself tells the story. There is no analogous phrase
for men.

It wasn't coercion, as in rape or other violence, that marked
relations between men and women during this period of the
sexual revolution. Rather, it was the coercive force of a movement that, in fact, had wide appeal to women, while it also rested
on a deeply entrenched structure of roles and relationships that
was bound to corrupt the ideals on which it was founded. For
sex does not stand alone, an activity isolated from other social,
cultural and institutional forces in our lives. The inequality in
gender relations permeates every aspect of life, influencing if
not determining women's decisions about such disparate life
situations as what kind of work they'll do and whether they'll
enter into a sexual relationship.

Saying yes or no, therefore, was no simple matter of individual
choice for a woman. The sexual ethos of the moment played its
part, to be sure. But the new standards developed against the
background of the old inequities in the social-sexual relations
between women and men. Thus, although the sexual revolution
did achieve some redistribution of goods—that is, a new distribution of sexual pleasure to include women more fully—it took
the gender revolution, which followed it and was partly a response to it, to begin the realignment of the structure of power
between men and women, both in bed and out of it.[5]

Yet a force had been let loose that would not be stilled, and
the revolution galloped along, spreading quickly to every corner
of the land. Undoubtedly, the eagerness with which women and
men grasped at the newfound opportunities for sexual expression
was a response to the repression that had been with us for so

long. But the fires were fed by the prospect of the huge profits to be made in the business of sex. Thus sex, which had been part of the consumer culture for decades, became bigger business than ever before, the obsession of the age. Here was another of the paradoxical aspects of the sexual revolution. On the one hand, sex was trivialized, stripped of symbolic content and meaning, of emotion and relatedness. On the other, it was invested with enormous importance, something to be pursued with unswerving persistence, as if it alone could resolve the problems of living in these difficult and uncertain times.

By the time the decade of the seventies reached center stage, the singles bars, which dotted the landscape in cities across the land, came to embody this contradiction. The media portrayed these bars as the playgrounds of the highly educated, young urban professionals—an image that still lives in the popular imagination. But, in fact, they attracted women and men from various sectors of the population, from doctors, lawyers, engineers and corporate executives to hairdressers, truck drivers, secretaries and assembly-line workers.

Certainly, there were upscale places that catered largely to a professional crowd, partly because only they could afford the prices there, partly because the ambience in these trendy spots intimidated others. But most singles bars had a relatively heterogeneous clientele—young people who may have seemed alike to the casual observer because they dressed, danced, ate and drank alike but who, in fact, were quite diverse in class, educational attainment and ethnic background.

Among the adults in this study, it generally wasn't class, education or occupation that differentiated those who went to singles bars from those who didn't. Rather, the distinguishing feature was more likely to be the social world a person lived in and identified with. Thus, for example, a woman who actively defined herself as a feminist and who socialized in those circles was less likely to be found in a singles bar than one who was more neutral on the subject. I don't mean to suggest, however, that the former was any less sexually active or any more discriminating in her choice of sexual partners than the latter, only that she found those partners elsewhere. For the singles bars were not the only places where casual sex flourished; they were only the most highly visible.

At the outset, the aim of most people who entered a bar probably was an innocent one, a place where men and women congregated to ease their loneliness and to have some fun. The tinkle of ice in hundreds of glasses, the music, the noise, the glitter, the laughter, the banter—all were magnets drawing single adults who, when work was finished, found themselves with many empty hours to fill. This was, after all, the first generation in which masses of unmarried young city dwellers lived outside the parental home, living alone or sharing quarters with others of their own age. With no family at hand, with many of their friends married and unavailable, with no community institutions or meeting places to support social life, no other places where singles gathered regularly, many found the bars a refuge to which they could retreat when they needed relief from the isolation of modern urban life.

Repeatedly, both men and women talked about going to a bar because they wanted to be in the presence of others like themselves, single people who were looking for some companionship, for a few hours of sociability. "If you were lonely and wanted some company, or even just to hear some music, that's where you went. There wasn't anyplace else then. Now there are some singles groups around—not that they're such great places to meet someone—or some people put ads in the paper. But after you check out those scenes a couple of times and you don't find what you're looking for, there's still no place else to go," explained 38-year-old Michael, a salesman from Philadelphia.

Whatever other reasons there may have been for the surging popularity of the singles bar during the 1970s, whatever a person's initial intent in going to them, they soon became what, in the language of the day, were called "meat racks." People may have come for sociability, but what they got was sex. "It's funny what happens," said 30-year-old Pete, a Cincinnati stockbroker who explained how, in the atmosphere of the singles bar, his thoughts quickly turn to sexual conquest. "You go there thinking maybe you'll meet someone you like, so you look around. You see someone attractive; you talk to them, and you know pretty quick it's not there. But do you leave and go on? No, you have a drink anyway; I don't know why, maybe because you don't want to be rude and hurt her. And then, before you know it, you're not thinking about the person; you're thinking only about the body. They lose all sense of being a person to you. Instead, you're stimulated by trying to figure out how you're going to make this happen. And that becomes life for the next five or six hours."

"Recreational sex" we were calling it by then—sex that was no more important than a handshake, impersonal, effortless, uncomplicated. But if recreation means fun, there seemed to be little of it around. Instead, all through the seventies and into the eighties, there was a kind of frantic sexuality, fleeting meetings and couplings that left people wanting. "Sex like that can be the most unintimate thing in the world. When it's over you feel empty and used," shuddered 40-year-old Donna as she recounted those experiences.

Even men who can count their one-night stands in three digits spoke eloquently about the emptiness of the experience, about all the times they were left feeling deprived and depleted. "I still do it once in a while, even though I know it's not worth it. It's not fun or stimulating anymore. When it's over, I feel kind of—what's the word?—wasted or empty, or something like that. I promise myself I'll turn over a new leaf and never walk into a bar again, but then I get drawn back in," said 34-year-old Sam, an optician from Pasadena. "I'm not really that kind of a guy; I want to be in a relationship with a woman I care about. That's the only time sex really means anything."

Why do they continue to do it, then?

Whether they meet in a singles bar or elsewhere, some people, more often men than women, undoubtedly engage in relatively transient, casual sex simply because sexual need asserts itself and the bed at home is empty. For them, the sexual gain outweighs whatever the emotional loss. "You know that Woody Allen line, 'Sex without love is an empty experience, but as empty experiences go, it's not bad.' Well, that's the truth," exclaimed a 36-year-old New York UPS driver, laughing.

But there are also other, more complicated reasons that keep people going back to experiences that give them so little satisfaction. For some, sex promises a moment of unconsciousness that brings respite from anxiety, pain, loneliness, boredom. Fleeting, perhaps, but effective in banishing these unwanted feelings, in allowing some surcease from the discomfort they inflict. The rise of sexual excitement pushes aside anxiety and boredom; the body contact, the sense of connection with another, assuages the pain and loneliness. "I wind up going into one of the bars because I get so damned lonely," said Kyle, a 33-year-old Memphis carpenter, with an apologetic smile. "Maybe it doesn't feel so good afterwards, but while I'm with the woman, it's okay; it makes me feel better. Not even just the sex but, you know, just having another body there."

For some, it's feeling and sensation they seek. But it's not a simple quest to have fun or to feel good. Rather, these tend to be people, more often men than women, who have become so distant from their feelings that they are numb, uncertain about whether they can feel at all. For them, the sensations of sex affirm their reality, helping them to know they're alive. "Sex is kicky and exciting, brings all the juices up to a boil," said a 36-year-old Phoenix real-estate broker, his voice rising in excitement as he explained its meaning to him. "Nothing makes you feel as . . . well, I don't know . . . alive, I'd guess you could say. You know, you feel kind of dead around the edges and you get up a good head of sexual steam and, wow, you're really living, man."

Then there are those, more often women than men, who experience their inner self as terrifyingly empty, a void which only the presence of another can fill. A sexual offering is the most dependable way to ensure that presence, enabling them to hold at bay the threat of wandering forever and alone in the abyss inside. "I don't do it anymore, but I know now that I traded sex for company a lot in those days," said 38-year-old Peggy, an accounting clerk in a Baltimore clothing factory. "I was so afraid to be alone. I actually had this feeling that I'd fall into some big black hole and never be able to get out. I used to tell myself I was very sexy, but I wasn't. I was just desperately needy."

Whatever motivates them to such casual sexual encounters, "empty" is the word both women and men use most frequently to describe their feelings about them. But despite this agreement, there also are important differences in what the experience means to each of them. Women usually enter these sexual interactions hoping for more. "If I take some guy home, it's because he seems okay and I think we might get something going," said 35-year-old Anne, an upholsterer in San Jose. "I don't think I'll ever get used to the fact that a guy leaves saying, 'I'll call you,' and you never hear from him again. You spend the night, even have sex that's promising sometimes, and then nothing, not a word. It always leaves me with a terrible feeling never to hear from them again."

"That's the problem with casual sex," said a 29-year-old New Jersey mechanic when we talked about why men don't call. "Someone always wakes up and thinks they're in a relationship. You know that, so you feel bad and say you'll call, but there's no reason to, so you forget about it."

The men almost universally say they are satisfied sexually in a one-night stand. Yes, there are those who tell of times when they couldn't sustain an erection and of the embarrassment and anxiety they felt then. But these generally are isolated moments, not the common or dominant experience for men. Conversely, women rarely report having orgasms in a transient encounter and most say they think it's of little concern to men. "No, I don't think I ever had an orgasm in a one-night stand, at least not with someone I just met," said 36-year-old Marjorie, a nurse in a New York hospital. "It's different with someone you know, like a guy who's a friend. Then a one-nighter can be fine, you know, where two people care about each other. But those other relationships, if you can call them that, aren't set up for that. Those guys think they're showing they care when they ask 'Was it good for you, too?' when it's all over."

Why is it that way? Why is male and female sexuality so differently constellated? What is it that generally makes it so easy for a man to find sexual satisfaction in an encounter with little or no sensual or emotional content, while it is so difficult for a woman?

We know, of course, that the cultural commandments about male and female sexuality not only shape our sexual behavior but affect the very way we experience our sexuality. For culture both clarifies and mystifies. A set of beliefs enables us to see the world more clearly at the same time that it blinds us to alternative visions. So, for example, Victorian women often shut out and denied the sexual messages their own bodies sent in order to bring their internal experience into line with the sexual mores of the day.

But this is not yet the whole story. Although the blueprint to which our sexuality conforms is drawn by the culture, the dictates of any society are reinforced by its institutional arrangements and mediated by the personal experience of the people who must live within them. And it is in this intersection of social arrangement and psychological response that we can see why sex and emotion come together so differently for women and men. All of which takes us back again to the family of childhood and to the attachments and identifications we make there.

At the beginning, our attachments are much deeper and more all-embracing than anything we, who have successfully buried that primitive past in our unconscious, can easily grasp. Their root is pure Eros, that vital, life-giving force that seeks connection with others and with which all attachment begins. But we are a society of people who have learned to look on Eros with apprehension, if not outright fear. For us, it is associated with passion, with sex, with forces that shout danger because they seem to be out of our control. This, I believe, is what makes the very *idea* of Eros seem so dangerous to family life, what motivates us to confine and contain it. Consequently, our young learn very early, and in ways too subtle and numerous to recount, about the need to limit the erotic, about our fears that Eros imperils civilization.

As the child grows past the early union with mother, therefore, the social norms about sexuality begin to make themselves felt. In conformity with those norms, the erotic and the emotional are split one from the other, and the erotic takes on a more specifically sexual meaning. For a boy at this stage, it's the emotional component of the attachment to mother that comes under attack as he seeks to repress his identification with her. The erotic—or sexualized—aspect of the attachment is left undisturbed, at least in heterosexual men. The incest taboo, of course, assures that future sexual *behavior* will take place with a woman other than mother. But I am not referring to behavior here. Rather, I'm speaking of the emotional structure that underlies it and that explains why, for a man, the erotic aspect of any relationship is the most compelling.

It isn't that men are not moved by emotion or that they can live comfortably without an intimate connection with another. But because of the particular way sex and emotion were severed in early childhood, in adulthood most men are perfectly capable of satisfying sexual need in encounters largely or wholly devoid of emotional connection.

For a girl, the developmental requirement is just the opposite. For her, it's the erotic component of the attachment to a woman that must be denied and shifted later to a man; the larger emotional involvement and identification remain intact. As a woman, therefore, the emotional aspect of a relationship will always be more vital, and she usually needs some kind of an emotional connection for sex to be wholly satisfying. "For sex to really work for me, I need to feel an emotional *something*," said 30-year-old Debby, a Los Angeles psychologist. "Without that, it's just another athletic activity, only not as satisfying, because when I swim or run, I feel good afterward."

Again, I am not speaking here of the behavior itself but of what motivates it and of the way it is experienced. Nor am I saying that a woman needs to be in love in order to find gratification in a sexual relationship with a man. Far from it. But before she can be sexually satisfied, she usually needs to believe she's in a relationship, however fleeting, and that there's some emotional connection, however small. True, it may exist only in her fantasy, but because she imbues it with this meaning, it is real for her. This is why she feels so disappointed when, after having sex with a man, he doesn't call again. For her, it was more than sex; it was a connection made, then lost.

Despite the fact that women so often found these transient encounters unsatisfying sexually, as the decade of the seventies wore on, sex as part of the evening's entertainment became more and more commonplace. "God, it's a little shocking when I remember some of the things I did then," said a 35-year-old corporate executive in Houston, a faint blush coloring her cheeks. "I was in college and this guy came to visit one of my roommates, but she wasn't home. So we hung out and talked for a while, then he lit a joint, and we smoked it, and next thing—I don't even know how it came about—I was giving him a blow job. I think about it now, and I can't believe I did things like that. But that's hindsight. Then I thought it was cool; he was just another one to add to the head count."

Seduction, which had been so much a part of the dating and mating scene just a decade earlier, all but disappeared. People met, spent a few hours and wound up in bed. Sometimes it was the beginning of a relationship; more often it was not. "It was just what you did, especially in college," 36-year-old Jim, a Phoenix landscape architect, said matter-of-factly as he recalled those early-seventies years. "It was easy to meet people because everybody was there together. So you'd go to a party or meet somebody in one of the coffee shops around the campus, and maybe you'd rap for a while, and pretty soon you'd go back to your place or hers, and that was it. Maybe once in a while you'd find somebody you really liked, and that was nice because then you'd go together for a while. But mostly that didn't happen, so you just had some good, friendly sex and went your way.

"It's still pretty much the same," he continued as he turned from past to present. "But now you have to go out of your way to meet someone, maybe make a date to see her. But it mostly always ends the same way."

"Good, friendly sex"—an experience that's not uncommon,

although for women, at least, it's rarely associated with a one-night stand with a stranger. About one-third of the women and men I interviewed told stories of having had sex with friends. Some said it was something they did once, when the moment was right. "I have this very good friend, Joe, and we were hanging out one day listening to some music, and I don't know why, it just happened," said Katy, a 27-year-old baker in Augusta. "We just looked at each other, and we both knew we were going to do it. It was really great, too."

"Yet you said you never did it again. Why?"

"I don't know exactly; I think maybe we were afraid of it, like maybe it would ruin this friendship if we really got into sex with each other. You know, that's powerful stuff. I love Joe, but like a friend, not somebody I want to be *in* love with."

Other people talked about having sex with a friend on some regular or periodic basis, what one woman called "platonic sex," by which she meant sex that fulfills sexual need and assuages loneliness but "isn't crazy, like romantic sex." "I've got a couple of good woman friends I spend time with, and when I'm not seeing someone and get lonely and horny, if one of them is free, too, we get together sexually," said 37-year-old Ben, a Boston salesman. "It's nice, no fireworks, but very, very nice. I think it's good for both of us. It kind of takes the edge off, and then you don't get desperate and do something stupid, like get involved with some person you know isn't going to be good for you."

All this sexual activity notwithstanding, neither men nor women are terribly satisfied with the other in bed. Some men complain that women are too aggressive now. "It's a pain in the ass with some women. They're so damned pushy about what they want, it feels like you're in bed with a traffic director," 26-year-old Eric, a brewery worker in Milwaukee, complained heatedly.

Others have the opposite complaint; women are too passive, they say. "Too many women just lay there like lumps, and you have to do all the work," groused 30-year-old Chris, a Louisville truck driver. "Nobody wants that. Sex is only really good when you have an active partner, somebody who's really involved and acts like she cares what's going on."

On their side, women of all ages and with diverse experiences insist that few men know much about making love to a woman. Sometimes the women spoke with patience and forbearance. A 29-year-old weaver from Boulder, Colorado, rested her cheek on her closed fist and sighed. "In some ways I understand why men are lousy lovers. How can you expect a guy to know what you're feeling when you have your clitoris stimulated? So maybe that's why so many of them are insensitive to a woman's needs. Even the good guys, like my boyfriend, they're run by their penis, not their brains or emotions. And when they're like that, nothing else counts," she concluded with a grimace and a gesture of futility.

Other women were brusque and intolerant. "I've had years of men who are lousy lovers. I don't know why I bother," said 35-year-old LuAnn, an Atlanta investment broker, her voice edged with disgust.

After hearing such remarks repeatedly, I commented to 25-year-old Deborah, a New York fitness trainer, "It's hard to believe there are so many men who are incompetent lovers. Surely by now most men know enough about a woman's anatomy to be reasonably good at it."

"Sure," she replied, her voice rising with anger and impatience, "if you mean that they know what buttons to push and think that's all they have to do. It's like they have a little ritual. They give you a touch here, a finger there, and a lick somewhere else, but there's nothing sensuous or sensual about it. It's just something they have to do to you to get you to do what they want to them. That's what they're really interested in, what *they're* feeling, not what's happening to you."

Men, having heard these complaints often enough, respond furiously. "It really pisses me off the way women think about men. I don't think being a good lover is based on some sort of technical understanding but on passion. People of both sexes respond to intensity and enthusiasm and, if not love, at least to the appearance of being very turned on," said a 39-year-old

Boston editor, the words falling from his lips urgently, as he sought to defend men from the stereotypic view so many women hold. "In fact, I think I care too much about what a woman feels, so that I often limit my own pleasure. Also, it becomes so important to me that I sometimes make a woman who doesn't have orgasms easily feel self-conscious about it, as if I were attacking a problem and turning the whole thing into some kind of clinical experience."

Indeed, most men insist that a woman's sexual fulfillment is important to them, that they feel best when the woman they're with has had an orgasm. "A lot of women say they don't care if they come or not. I don't like it when that happens; I feel like I'm out there by myself in a way. She's what I call the rag doll; I just strap her on and dance with her, but she's not involved. Who needs *that?*" asked a 40-year-old Washington chef with a dismissive wave of his hand.

"I look at it as the challenge of sexual intercourse," he continued. "When you satisfy her, it's not just that you've given her pleasure, but you've done something for yourself, too. It's very hard to understand it when a woman says, 'That's okay, I don't need to come.' I just can't understand why she wouldn't feel the same need I have. Why would she be having sex if she doesn't want to get that great feeling?"

Surely this is part of the problem: men and women who come together sexually for very different reasons. For him, it's sex that's paramount. He may want to be held and touched as much as she, but the frustration would be intolerable without the release of orgasm. For her, the sensual is inseparable from the sexual, and orgasm generally depends on the nature of the whole experience. "Some men obviously have learned that it's not all in the penis entering the vagina where the action happens," said Dawn, a 38-year-old personnel manager. "But what drives me crazy is that they're not very creative about it. They make a beeline for the clitoris, and pretty soon there's this feeling of 'Well, I've been doing this now for about three minutes, are you going to have an orgasm, or what?' When that happens, I know I'm not going to come, so I say forget it and try to enjoy the physical contact. I don't understand why men aren't more sensual, or maybe it's just that whatever sensuality they have is in their penis. All I know is that most of the men I've known seem insensitive to a woman's need for that kind of sensuality as part of sex."

On their side, some men, at least, talk of feeling confused about women's sexual needs and intimidated by their demands. They try, they say. They have a satisfying and successful experience with a woman and think they learned something they can rely on. So they set about putting that knowledge into practice, only to find themselves accused of, as one man said, "playing it by the numbers." "It amazes me how radically different women's sexual responses are. It changes from one woman to the next so much that it doesn't make it easy to be a good lover," explained a 38-year-old San Francisco photographer, his head shaking, his words echoing the bewilderment in his eyes. "If you've had an experience where you felt successful and the woman agreed that you were a good lover, you can't just transfer that repertoire to your next relationship because that new woman may respond very differently. The one real common denominator I've observed is that most women find the foreplay and afterplay at least as important as what comes in between."

Undoubtedly men as well as women want an erotic, engaged, tender experience, sex that's not just goal-directed but pleasure-directed as well. But when talking about a partner's satisfaction, men often make a distinction between casual sex and sex in a relationship. Some men said it baldly, without embarrassment or apology. "Hell, I wasn't concerned with mutual orgasm. What did I care about them? It was hash marks on my arm, like a fighter pilot with notches in the gun butt," blurted out 37-year-old Carl, a New York salesman.

Others spoke with less force and more sensitivity. "Of course it's important to me for a woman to have an orgasm," said 34-year-old Guy, an engineer in Columbus. "The whole thing's a team effort as far as I'm concerned. She's not there for me alone, and to the extent she's putting a smile on my face, I want to do the same for her."

"Is that true even in a one-night stand?"

"Good point! I'm much less inclined to care one way or the other then, but that's the nature of the relationship."

This, then, may be at least part of the reason why women complain so much about men in bed. A man who might be a fine lover in a relationship may not care very much when he's in a casual sexual encounter. He's pleased if his partner is satisfied sexually, since there's a good deal of ego gratification in it for him. So he may make some effort to try to make it happen. But it's limited compared with what he's willing to put out with a woman he cares about.

I found some confirmation for this speculation in the fact that the few women who were willing to give men high marks as lovers either had never engaged in casual sex or had forsworn it long ago. "I haven't had the experience of getting stuck with lousy lovers in quite a few years," said 43-year-old Judy, a Cambridge psychologist. "But maybe that's because I gave up going to bed with people I didn't really care about and who didn't care about me. Now I only pursue sex with someone where there's some common ground and a mutual erotic urge. I don't mean it has to be a great relationship, but it has to have some emotional substance to it. When you've got that, you can forget about lousy lovers. So the men I tend to be with now are always very satisfactory lovers; some of them have even been great."

Men aren't the only ones who say they aren't concerned about a partner's pleasure in a transient encounter, however. When talking to women about how they feel when they meet temporary impotence in men, for example, several said much the same thing. "When I was having casual sex, I didn't want to be bothered with any trouble," explained Louise, a 42-year-old Minneapolis professor, with an impatient toss of her head. "I didn't want any limp erections, and I didn't want to have to work at it. If it wasn't perfect, I didn't want any part of it. It worked or it didn't, and I didn't want to have to do anything to help it along. If you care about someone, it's different. Then it's okay if it's not perfect, and I'll do what I have to to make it better."

Men, on the other hand, generally say that women are "wonderful," "sweet," "gentle," "kind," "tender" when they have problems with getting or maintaining an erection. "Sometimes, when it's someone I just met, or it's the first time even with someone I know, I have some trouble getting it up," said Dan, a 35-year-old computer technician from the Silicon Valley. "It feels like shit when that happens, but I've never been with a woman who isn't very nice about it, real sweet."

Most women agree that the sight of a limp penis brings a rush of sympathy to their hearts and reassuring words to their mouths. "It isn't that I care whether he's satisfied or not. Who worries about that with a man? If they can get it up, they're satisfied. But when they can't, you know that it's the hardest thing a guy has to face, so you can't help feeling sorry for him and trying to make it okay," said 27-year-old Lynne, a Pittsburgh police-woman. "Sometimes when it happens a guy puts on an act, but you can tell he's sick about it and scared to death about his manhood. I never can figure out why what his prick is doing—or not doing, I should say—is so damned important to a guy. Can you?"

As we discussed the details of their sexual history, about half the women—more among those who were products of the sixties than those who came later—spoke of regrets, of wishing they could take it back, do it over again. Some women said they hoped their lover or husband would never find out the details of their sexual past. "I wouldn't want my husband ever to know what I did in my promiscuous phase, never, because I don't want him to think about me that way," said Marsha, a 37-year-old Berkeley lawyer.

"What way?" I asked.

"Cheap. Things haven't changed that much, you know. Whatever he did was fine, but a woman, that's different. Yeah, yeah, I know all about these guys who say it's not true. But when it's *their* woman, they sing a different tune. I feel cheap when I think about it, so how else could he feel? I mean, he knew I wasn't the queen of the virgins, but he doesn't know about all this stuff we're talking about now."

"My promiscuous phase"—not words a man would use to

describe such a period in his life. He might say he was "sleeping around a lot," or "fucking around," or "sticking it to every woman he could find," or any other of a dozen expressions, vulgar or not, that would make the point. But the word "promiscuous" wouldn't be his, since it virtually always is associated with a woman's sexual behavior, not a man's.[6]

Interesting, isn't it, that even though more than two and a half decades have passed since the sexual revolution brought women a new measure of sexual freedom, there's still no word in the language that doesn't reek with pejorative connotation to describe a woman who has sex freely. Since language frames thought and sets its limits, this is not a trivial matter. For without a word that describes without condemning, it's hard to think about it neutrally as well. When we say the words "promiscuous woman," therefore, it's a statement about her character, not just her sexual behavior.

Partly because of the meaning attached to promiscuity, for those who are still single, regret is mixed with bitterness and resentment, especially among women who continue to search for a permanent relationship in the face of declining hope. "I could have done without sleeping with a lot of those people," said Candace, a 39-year-old Chicago graphic artist, passing a hand over her face as if to cover the pain that was visible there. "God, how I wish I hadn't! If I knew then . . . Well, what's the use? I didn't."

"Why the regrets? Nothing has been lost, has it?"

"Yes, it has. Sex is supposed to mean something, and not just be this transitory activity. Most of the time I wasn't really doing what I wanted to do. I'd have sex with someone because it seemed like it was easier to go through with it and do it than it was to say no and get out of the situation. Do you know what it feels like to wake up to some stranger from the night before and think: 'Oh God, why? What am I doing here?' The guy's happy, he feels like a conqueror, and you feel humiliated because you know you'll probably never hear from him again."

Almost always such words came from women who felt that they had exceeded some limit, that they had allowed themselves to be exploited far too long. But the claim made so often that "I wasn't really doing what I wanted to do" seems to represent a retrospective reworking of yesterday in light of feelings and events today, a simplification of the complex and ambivalent set of emotions that governed their behavior then. For it is both true and not true: true in the sense that all the pressures of the day made it harder to say no than to say yes; not true because there was something women were looking for in these encounters, something they needed and wanted, perhaps something they feared they couldn't get without sex.

Partly there was simply the wish to join the adventure, to let go of the restraints inside them. "There was excitement all around, all your friends doing these adventurous things sexually. It was hard to resist; sometimes you didn't want to, even though there was stuff inside you saying, 'Don't,' " said 41-year-old Jill, a Portland bank manager.

Partly there was the need to test themselves, to broaden the limits of their sexuality, to define it in ways that belonged to them, not to their mothers. "I just wanted to know who I was, what my sexuality meant to me, not to all those other people in the world who'd been telling me what it should mean all my life," said a 29-year-old sales supervisor from Tucson.

For many women the need to be touched, held, hugged, was paramount. "Touch is part of my way of being in the world, and when I'm not able to touch and be touched, I feel very deprived," commented 45-year-old Evelyn, a Detroit school counselor.

And overriding it all was the hope of establishing a more lasting relationship. "I always had the expectation that it would become a relationship, but obviously the men I was with had a different agenda," said 36-year-old Suzanne, a government worker in Washington.

The last said over and over again by women of all ages. Yet experience told them that "the expectation that it would become a relationship" was not likely to be met. Why, then, did they continue to do it? The ability to deny what we don't want to see is common to all of us. In this case, the denial of their own experiences served to allow them to continue to enter sexual

relationships that somewhere inside they knew would be nothing
more. But the question remains: Why did they need to hold on
to the belief? Here, it seems to me, that along with whatever
other needs motivated them, the cultural mores about women
and sex play their part. In an earlier generation, women convinced themselves they were in love in order to have sex before
marriage. In an age of greater sexual freedom, they only have
to believe they're at the beginning of a relationship.

The women who live with regrets are only one part of the
story, however. A roughly equal number look back positively
on their sexual past. "There was the period when I was very
sexually active and slept with people I maybe saw twice before,"
recalled 39-year-old Barbara, a Minneapolis investment broker.
"But when I think back on it, I never made bad choices. I wasn't
indiscriminate and didn't have sex with anyone I happened to
meet walking down the street. If it wasn't someone I knew, he
was someone I knew something about. Looking back, I don't
think it ever got out of control like it did for a lot of people. I
sort of kept my feet on safe and solid ground, and I also had a
wonderful time exploring my sexuality and my personal limits."

Instead of regretting what they did, some of these women
lament what they *didn't* do. "All this talk you hear now that
people are sorry for what they did; I don't understand it," said
44-year-old Marie, the manager of a dress shop in Tacoma. "The
only thing I wish is that I could have been more open and less
inhibited then, but I didn't have the guts. Oh, I had plenty of
sex, but I missed out on a lot of good times and also the opportunity to explore all kinds of different sexual approaches because I was too inhibited. I think I'd have been happier and had
more real sexual pleasure if I'd used that period of my life more
fully and wisely. So maybe I'd have made a few mistakes, so
what?"

Still others look back with nostalgia, relishing thoughts of the
sexual excitement during those years of exploration and experimentation. "Everybody says sex in a relationship is more fulfilling. Well, maybe it is, or maybe I've been in the wrong
relationships," said a 40-year-old New York designer. "But I'm

not sure about the trade-off. Too much of the carnality and kinkiness go out of sex in a relationship, and it's a lot less thrilling than casual sex, which is filled with expectation, excitement, mystery, fantasy—all the stuff that makes sex so wonderful."

Some of the women who speak positively of the past may also examine their early experiences with a critical eye. But at the same time, they insist that they wouldn't do anything differently if they had it to do over again. "I feel so lucky I came of age after the Pill and before AIDS," said 42-year-old Katherine, a Berkeley professor. "From this perspective, that looks like the one shining moment of *Camelot*. The only things I would have done differently are more, not less. I regret not living out a fantasy or two. But mostly I'm just grateful for that period and the things I learned then.

"Sure, there was a dark side; it wasn't all roses. But there were also wonderful, exciting times. Of course, I wouldn't mind being a 20-year-old with the understanding of a 42-year-old. Who would? But I got to be the person I am now by living through that period as a 20-year-old. It was all part of the job description."

What distinguishes these women from those who speak with regret? What makes some say they "wouldn't trade those experiences for anything," while others talk about wishing they "could take it back"?

Certainly individual psychology plays a part. Those who see a half-empty glass are more likely to live with regret than those who see the glass half full. Women who, however they acquired it, have a sense of entitlement, for whom the words "I deserve" don't evoke guilt or anxiety, will tend to experience the pleasure more keenly than the pain.

Beyond these distinctly individual differences, however, there are those that are related to where people place themselves in the social world, what kind of social and political commitments have governed their lives. Women who identified with the women's movement in its early years, and who still consider themselves feminists now, are most likely to look back with satisfaction. Whether single or coupled, they usually feel that the years of sexual exploration were crucial in the development of a healthy sexuality and of an autonomous, bounded self they now can rely on. "Sure, I hear women carry on about that time, and I suppose I could bring up some angry emotions about some of the experiences I had, too—times when I was pushed and shoved into things I wouldn't have done if I'd had a better sense of who I was then," said 40-year-old Ruth, a Spokane journalist. "But I wouldn't take any of it back; it was all part of the process of figuring out a new context for your sexuality. At the beginning, women were doing it for men, just like they always had. We didn't know yet that only when you're doing it for yourself, then you can say you're sexually free. It took that experimenting around for women to develop a sense of self they could trust to make the right decision for them.

"We were the transition generation, and that's what happens when people are the first ones to live through a period of change. They tend to throw out the old altogether at first. Then after a while, they can start to figure out what to put back in and how they really want to live with the new. It's all part of the process of how we got to where we are now, so it was necessary."

"The transition generation"—not just a few of the intellectual elite but the first mass movement to try to bring real equality into the sexual realm, to insist that women have the right to sexual expression as fully and freely as men. The first, also, to insist on defining the borders of female sexuality themselves and to demand that men attend to both their definitions and their needs.

Until then, men had defined the vaginal orgasm as the "mature" female sexual response. The fact that few women could claim the experience gave most of the experts of the day little pause for thought. The theory wasn't wrong, women had a problem, they asserted confidently. If she wasn't fully satisfied with vaginal penetration alone, it was her failing. Her partner wasn't ignorant or inadequate; she was frigid. She had to be fixed, not he. Suddenly the young women of the sixties generation rose up and shouted, "No!" Suddenly, women who had been disconnected from their lived experience for so long were insisting on finding their way to it.

It was a bold experiment, daring and brave. There were problems and excesses, to be sure. And there were failures as well. But the sexual revolution they wrought has left its mark on succeeding generations, as each, in turn, has consolidated the gains of the last, while also continuing to expand the boundaries of sexuality in their time.

1. Todd Gitlin, *The Sixties: Years of Hope, Days of Rage* (New York: Bantam Books, 1987), p. 371.
2. See Norman O. Brown, *Life Against Death* (New York: Vintage Books, 1959); Herbert Marcuse, *Eros and Civilization* (Boston: Beacon Press, 1955) and *One-Dimensional Man* (Boston: Beacon Press, 1964); and Wilhelm Reich, *The Sexual Revolution* (New York: Noonday Press, 1962).
3. Gitlin, *The Sixties*, p. 372.
4. Gitlin, *The Sixties*. In a chapter on the emergence of a woman's voice in the New Left (pp. 362–376), Gitlin recounts the details of a January 1969 meeting in which women asked for and got a place on the agenda. When Marilyn Webb, a longtime member of Students for a Democratic Society, stood to talk about the oppression of women, she was met with shouts: "Take her off the stage and fuck her!" "Take her down a dark alley!" "Take it off."
5. For an important discussion of the issues raised here, see also Mariana Valverde, "Beyond Gender Dangers and Private Pleasures: Theory and Ethics in the Sex Debate," *Feminist Studies* 15, 2 (Summer 1989): 237–254. See also Ann Snitow, Christine Stansell and Sharon Thompson, eds., *Powers of Desire: The Politics of Sexuality* (New York: Monthly Review Press, 1983), and Carole S. Vance, ed., *Pleasure and Danger: Exploring Female Sexuality* (Boston: Routledge & Kegan Paul, 1984).
6. Only when a man is homosexual is the word "promiscuous" in common use. Then, perhaps because society wishes to restrain his sexual behavior just as it does the behavior of women, it gives it this pejorative label.

# 6

---·•·---

# Sex, Gender and Power

$A$s the decade of the eighties unfolded, some changes came into view—shifts that remain with us into the present. Most visible among them, the casual sex that had been so prominent earlier began to take second place to sex in a relationship. It isn't that there are no longer any one-night stands, no near-anonymous fleeting encounters, only that the dominant ethos, and the values men and women now give voice to, call for sex between two people who have some kind of emotional connection, even if it's a relatively transient one.

Yet it's a complicated code, one that's probably violated almost as often as it's honored. A one-night stand with a friend is acceptable; with a stranger it's looked upon askance, although certainly not uncommon. The emotional connection that's supposed to be a prerequisite to a sexual one need not be a substantial or lasting one. Liking someone is enough to justify spending a night or a weekend, even on the first meeting. And many, if not most, of the young women who remain virgins feel they're carrying a burden, one they'll be glad to lay aside. Thus, while change from the over-35 generation is undeniable, it's more of a subtle shift in emphasis rather than a dramatic reversal of form.

Not surprisingly, also, where social values have been so deeply internalized, some conflicts remain, and change in consciousness often lags well behind the changed behaviors. The mystery of sex, the symbolic meanings with which we have invested it, the ways in which it has come to define us as man and woman, feminine and masculine, the balance of power between us—all these are at stake in our changing sexual relations. Consequently, change and resistance live alongside each other, women and men savoring newfound freedoms in one moment and conflicted about them in the next. We *do* new things; we *say* new words. But words alone cannot change feelings, and the internal emotional response is sometimes at odds with the external behavioral one.

Still, as I have already suggested, language and consciousness are not unrelated. Quite the contrary. Language frames thought and, as such, it is often the forerunner to the kind of internal change that allows us to live more comfortably with the changing behavior. New ways of being come to our attention; we name them and, even if we don't act upon them at once, a new sense of the possible exists inside us, a new dimension, a new way of seeing the world, perhaps of being in it.

There is no better example of how this happens than the sexual revolution, which, along with its companion, the gender revolution, has profoundly changed the way we think about sex and gender. In giving us a new language with which to consider the role of women in society, these two social movements opened the possibility for change in arenas of living that, until they erupted, most people assumed had long been settled. But even when we are eager for change, none of it happens without resistance. For change threatens the existing balance, a threat that's not taken lightly either by the external social world or by the internal psychological one.

For men, especially, the sexual freedom of women, which has

given them so much pleasure, has also had its price. No longer can they claim exclusive rights to the woman of their choice. No longer can they alone define the boundaries of female sexual expression. At one level, most men give assent to these new sexual realities. "I think it's only fair; a woman's got the same rights as a man." At another level, sometimes unconscious, sometimes not, their responses range from ambivalence to downright hostility. "I know it's weird; it's just a stupid, stereotypic way of thinking about how girls are supposed to be," Jeremy, a 21-year-old Boston student, said self-consciously. "I'm against it consciously, but it's hard for me to deal with the fact that a girl would be as sexually active as me, or maybe more so. It's something real powerful deep inside me, and I can't push it away no matter how hard I try."

When I asked men if they ever wished women were less sexually available, they almost invariably answered with an unequivocal "No." But it wasn't long before they were also complaining about women who are "too sexually aggressive," who are "too easy," who want to "hop into bed," who "come on too strong sexually," who "think you're queer if you don't happen to feel like it." Or they lamented the fact that, as one man said, "It's a whole different game now, not so exciting. There's no challenge anymore."

It seems, then, that although most men no longer dream of virgins in their bed, the alternatives are troubling. "I used to think I wanted to marry a virgin, but I've outgrown that," said Jon, a 25-year-old Cleveland repairman, his discomfort at the admission evident in the way his shoulders tensed and his eyes dropped to the floor. "That was one of the big hang-ups with Jamie, who was the only girl I was ever in love with. She had sex with only one guy before me, but I couldn't really accept it, so I used it to hurt her sometimes. We had a great sex life. She was great about doing me and letting me come in her mouth, but I just couldn't stand to think she did that with anybody else."

Women respond with angry exasperation. "I sometimes think what men really want now is a sexually experienced virgin," exploded 21-year-old Claire, a student in Madison, Wisconsin, as she fairly jumped out of her chair and began to pace the room. "They want you to know the tricks, but they don't like to think you did those things with anyone else."

For many of the women in their twenties, the answer to this male ambivalence is to do what women have done for ages. They evade the truth, if they don't outright lie. But it's not without cost to their sense of integrity. "I'd never tell my boyfriend how many guys I've slept with," said 21-year-old Carla, a New York secretary, who put the number at twelve. "It upsets me that I can't be honest about it because it's not the way I want this relationship to be. But I know he'd feel terrible about it because I've heard how he talks about other girls. I don't want him to think I'm a slut, because it's not true. I never really did any of those one-night-stand things. It was always with a guy I was going with."

In a questionnaire survey I distributed to 600 students in eight colleges around the country, almost 40 percent of the sexually active women, many of them less experienced than Carla, said they understate their sexual experience because "my boyfriend wouldn't like it if he knew," "people wouldn't understand," "I don't want him to think I'm a slut."

Most are angry about this need to dissemble. "It pisses me off that men can still define what's okay and not okay for me to do." But some accept it without much reaction, one of the realities of life. "It's just the way it is, so I don't tell and don't bother myself about it."

I wondered at first whether the women had misjudged the men, whether they were acting on assumptions that were no longer valid. But I soon found that they understood the situation all too well. In reply to a question about what they expected of the woman they might marry, well over half the men commented that they wouldn't want a woman who had been "around the block too many times"; that they were looking for someone who didn't "sleep around"; that a woman who did was "a slut"—the definition being what it has been for most of this century, a woman whose sexual activity is no more, most likely far less, than a man's.

It's clear, then, that while the ground over which it is now being fought has changed dramatically, the struggle for sexual equality has not yet been fully won. Men still hold the power to define the acceptable; women still conceal their sexual behavior. But it's no small change that many, if not most, men now question the legitimacy of their own thoughts and feelings and that most women are now angry about such sexual inequities.[1]

Whatever the residue of the past, whatever the conflicts and ambivalences may be, sex undoubtedly has become more varied, more adventurous, and freer for both men and women. Women, in particular, are in closer touch with the sexual part of themselves and freer to act upon it than at any time in this century. Thus, for example, faking orgasm, a relatively common practice as late as the early 1970s, when I was doing the research for an earlier book,[2] is much more rare today. Then, over 70 percent of the women I spoke with said they faked orgasm at least some of the time. Now, the same proportion says, "Never." Instead, once they have had some sexual experience, most women today expect to have orgasms when they're in a relationship and say they feel able to let their partner know how to help make it happen. When it doesn't, they feel under no compulsion to put on an act.

In the early seventies, oral sex was, as I have already said, a source of conflict between many of the married couples I interviewed. Working-class women generally called the practice "disgusting," and few willingly engaged in it. Among the college-educated middle class, women were more likely to participate in oral sex, but most did so only to please their husbands. Now all surveys show that both attitude and behavior have shifted markedly, and cunnilingus and fellatio are practiced by 90 percent of the people responding—not just among those in coupled relationships but among singles as well. In the research for this book, about three-fourths of the college students who responded to the questionnaire said they engaged in oral sex. Among the people with whom I did face-to-face interviews, every single one had at least some experience with it, and most said it was a routine part of their repertoire of sexual behaviors.

Of all the possibilities in heterosexual sex, the two ways women said they come to orgasm most easily are with cunnilingus or when they are on top. There are, of course, still some women who resist a lover's attempts at cunnilingus. Some are put off by negative feelings about their own body. "Ugh, I just don't feel like it's clean enough there." Others insist that most men don't really want to do it and that they feel too uncomfortable to go ahead when they sense resistance. "It seems to me they want it done to them, but they don't feel comfortable giving it. Who wants to be in the position of asking someone to do something that repels them?"

While this undoubtedly is true for some men, most of those I spoke with maintained that they generally have no problem with cunnilingus, often saying they found it pleasurable and exciting. But here, too, they make a clear separation between casual sex and sex in a relationship. "I'm not about to feel like I want to go down on some woman I don't really know, I mean, someone I just met," said 29-year-old Matt, a Portland psychologist. "I don't know why she'd expect it in a one-night stand. It's too intimate; it doesn't fit with the situation. So, sure, when she indicates, however she does that, that it's what she wants, I won't jump to do it. But when I'm with a woman I know and care about, it's no problem at all."

As for fellatio, women sometimes complained about men's preoccupation with it. "It seems like every man I've ever known, all he could think of was a blow job." Some women talked about "not liking that thing in my mouth"; said that "it makes me feel like I'm choking"; worried that "the whole thing doesn't feel clean." But the responses of most of the women in this study ranged from "No problem" to "It's fine" to "I love it"—the last most common among the 18–34-year-olds.

When I asked the women who responded most enthusiastically to elaborate, they usually spoke first of the joy of giving a partner pleasure. "I just love to do it because it makes him so happy; it makes me feel good to do that for him," said Becky, a 25-year-old Louisville nursery-school teacher. But as they warmed to the subject, they spoke far more passionately about how powerful they felt when performing fellatio. "It's the ultimate power," she continued, with a Machiavellian grin. "I know some women who don't like it and say it feels like they're getting something jammed down their throat. But for me, it's sort of like having him tied up. He's just lying there getting more and more excited and praying you won't stop. When a guy's penis is in my mouth, he's absolutely, totally vulnerable. It's the one time I'm totally in control."

The men, however, had their own version of the same event. For them, too, the issue was power. But it was they who felt powerful when on the receiving end of fellatio. "I love it; it feels great," said a 32-year-old Los Angeles executive, one hand slapping the air for emphasis as he talked. "But I have to admit, I get a feeling of real power, and that adds to the whole sexual thrill. When a woman puts my penis into her mouth, it's the ultimate act of submission."

When it comes to sex, power, it seems, depends as much upon the symbolic meanings, upon the way an act is perceived, as upon any hard-and-fast reality.

It's not just oral sex for which this is true, but for many of the variety of positions as well. So, for example, being on top was mentioned by many women as the preferred position, not just because more clitoral stimulation is possible this way, but because they feel most in control. "I like it best when I'm on top. I could think of all kinds of reasons why, but I think the big reason is because it makes me feel as if I keep the power, and I'm the one who's in control of what both of us are doing," said 19-year-old Andrea, a postal clerk from Richmond. Then hesitating, as if uncertain about whether to say more, she continued: "Mostly, I don't feel as much that I'm being penetrated."

"What about being penetrated is an issue?"

"I don't know exactly. I think maybe it's because I feel too vulnerable when I'm on my back. It feels . . . feels . . . penetrated; there's no other word for it. It's like I'm pinned or nailed or something like that. In that position, there's nothing I could do to protect myself. He has all the power and all you can do is accept it. It's too passive."

For women, the issues are power and control, penetration and submission. For many men, however, it's a relief to be able to assume the more passive posture at least some of the time, to be freed from the sense of total responsibility that accompanies sex in the more traditional missionary position. "It's a real pleasure when a woman takes charge of sex sometimes," said 28-year-old Dean, a factory foreman in Detroit. "Too many women still expect you to do it all. It gets to be a pain in the ass to be responsible for the whole thing all the time. The woman I'm seeing now is real active, and she loves to be on top, so I can relax and enjoy it. It's a big relief."

The relationship between sex and power is a difficult one for most people to deal with directly, since they prefer to maintain the romantic imagery about sex as solely a loving and intimate contact. "Making love," for example, is the phrase people most commonly use to talk about all sexual encounters, many of them anything but loving. When I would comment on the discrepancy between the words and the reality, as I often did in an interview, people generally would shift uncomfortably in their chairs, laugh self-consciously, drop their gaze, or send any one of a number of other signals of their discomfort at having to confront what they undoubtedly already knew. Yet they continued to use the language of love, suggesting, it seems to me, that this enabled them to justify behavior they might otherwise have to question.

Still, it's virtually impossible to have any extended conversation about sex without tripping over the issue of power, although often it's named something else. For, in fact, the bedroom is one of the primary places where men and women meet as intimate adversaries, where unspoken negotiations go on as they seek to get something they want—to gain an edge, to get control, to feel more powerful in relation to the other. Women, for example, sometimes talked about using sex to hurt a partner. "More than once I've used sex to hurt people I was involved with," said 34-year-old Wendy, a cook in Boulder. "It's a way of getting back some control in a relationship when you feel you might have lost it. I'd get sexually involved with someone else just because I knew how much it would hurt the guy I was with. I'm not proud of those times, but I have to admit that I felt a sense of triumph."

Other women either withheld sex altogether or, more subtly, withheld orgasm. "There's not a lot a woman can do to a man, but one way to get him is not to have an orgasm," laughed 26-year-old Paulette, a TV production assistant in Philadelphia, who masturbated to orgasm easily and regularly. "I know, I know, it sounds terrible, but it's true. Since my first boyfriend in high school broke up with me, I've never come with a man, only when I'm masturbating. I've been with this guy for a few months now, and it makes him crazy because he feels inadequate and like he's doing something wrong. He keeps trying, but I just can't; I can't help it."

"Can't or won't?" I asked.

"Call it what you want," she snapped. "I don't."

For men, the issue of a woman's orgasm raises a complicated set of feelings and motivations. Undeniably, most men want a partner to find pleasure and satisfaction in the sexual interaction. Many, in fact, insist that when a woman doesn't, their own pleasure is diminished substantially. But it's also true that their sense of self and manhood is attached to their ability to make it happen, to be, as one man put it, "the author of a woman's orgasm." Or, as 27-year-old Fred, a Boston bus driver, explained: "If I'm with a woman who can have an orgasm with anybody, I like it that she does, but it doesn't feel that important to me because it doesn't have anything to do with me. But with other women who can't do it so easily, that's something else. Then it's a challenge to make it happen, and when it does, there's no finer compliment I can get. It makes me feel powerful, strong—I guess you could say macho—to think I'm the reason she's having this orgasm."

For some men, it's also a matter of raw power. "You have to remember, there are two ways to subjugate women," said Ken, a 35-year-old Augusta TV technician, his broad smile meant to soften his words. "One is to fuck them and leave them. The other is more crafty, but it's the real power number—making sure they have an orgasm so that they'll be bound to you."

"Why would you think that would bind a woman?"

"Come on, you know why. I'll bet you've heard plenty about what lousy lovers we men are. Baby, when you know how to be a good lover, you can keep them coming back time after time."

Anal sex, too, raises the issue of dominance and submission very sharply for most people. To the degree that it's part of the sexual repertoire, it's much like oral sex was a couple of decades ago. Mostly, although not universally, men are asking for it, women resisting it. Some men for whom it's important say they like it simply because it feels good. "It's very tight, so you get very intense feelings."

Others talk about the sense of power it gives them. "I don't know, how can I explain it? It's aggressive; it's powerful, almost like caveman stuff, like throwing her on the bed on her belly and taking her and she can't move. That sounds a little kinky, I guess, but some women like it."

A few of the women I met agreed that they like being "taken" that way. "There's something exciting about it. Look, it's not that I have rape fantasies or anything like that, but there's a feeling of being mastered that's, I don't know, very stimulating."

A few others said it was just plain pleasurable. "It's a very special thrill that I can't really describe if you haven't felt it. I know lots of women don't like it, but if they could relax and let it happen, they'd know what I'm talking about."

Most of the women who had tried it, however, complained that it hurt too much, and they resented men who tried to push them into it. "I don't know what's supposed to be pleasurable about it; it hurts like hell. I have no patience for these guys who keep trying to convince you to do it; it makes me furious."

There presently are no reliable data on what proportion of the American people engage in anal sex, but experts in the field estimate that about 30 percent have at least tried it. Some investigations report figures that are much higher. In a 1983 survey of its readership, *Playboy* reported that 61 percent had anal sex.

One year later, *Self's* readers put the figure at 51 percent, up 13 percent from their 1980 study. My own data show that over one-third of today's college students have at least experimented with anal sex, while among the older people, close to half have had some experience with it—an extraordinary increase in the years since the early 1970s, when it was almost unheard of among heterosexuals.

Pornography, made more accessible by the advent of the videocassette recorder, has increasingly found its way into the lives of the respectable. Almost two-thirds of those who returned questionnaires and over half of those I interviewed said they sometimes used pornographic films as a sexual stimulant when they were in a relationship, even if it was only a brief one. The younger the age group, the more likely this was to be seen as an erotic option. Not a surprise, given that they were raised during both the sexual revolution and the technological revolution in video communication—the one leaving them with fewer inhibitions than their elders about all kinds of sexual behavior; the other putting a wide array of videotapes of all kinds at their disposal from the time they were small children.

Still, some things don't change. More often than not, the idea to watch an X-rated film comes from the man. "I'd never suggest doing it, but this boyfriend I used to have liked it, and I didn't mind, so I went along," said 19-year-old Naomi, a Connecticut student. "We never watched for very long; ten minutes and we would get turned on and never mind what they were doing."

Some of the women who "went along" said the films hold no interest at all for them.[3] "It doesn't do anything for me; it's like watching someone chew food or something," said 22-year-old Lisa, a Cambridge manicurist. Yet many who spoke such words watched because a "boyfriend likes to see them."

Women far more often than men called the films boring and unimaginative, yet many also found them arousing. "It always puzzles me that they can be so stimulating when they're so stupid and terrible," mused 30-year-old Kate, a Houston teacher. "The people who act in them are awful, and you don't have any sense that they want to be doing it. It's curious that watching people who don't want to do it stimulates our wanting to do it, isn't it? I don't understand it, but it's fun."

Few men talked about the exploitation of women in these films, but the women noticed and often objected, saying they found them offensive. "I think they're disgusting; it makes me very angry how they treat women in them," said 24-year-old Angela, a Charleston waitress.

Group sex, whether in a trio, a quartet, or some larger number, had been experienced by over one-fourth of both groups of respondents—that is, those who answered the questionnaire and those who were interviewed. "Yes, I've done it several times, once with seven people. I enjoyed it tremendously, although I also think it's a problem if some people in the group are coupled," said 41-year-old Gina, a department-store executive in Cleveland. "I don't care how liberated people are, they don't do well knowing their lover or mate is fucking somebody else right there in the room with them. Sure, I've heard people say they got turned on by seeing it, and maybe they do. But I think when they go home, something else happens. Anyway, I've never known a couple who survived doing much of that."

"What about you, what do you like about it?"

Laughing, "Boy, it was a long time ago. Let me think. You mean, besides it's fun. Well, first of all, there's the excitement of knowing you're doing something you're not supposed to be doing. I mean, when you do group sex, you're really breaking *all* the rules. And sexually it's great, all those bodies, and somebody doing something to different parts of you at the same time. Or you're sucking somebody off while somebody else is doing it to you. That's pretty hot stuff. Besides the actual sex, there's something else; I don't know if I can say it. I felt like I was free, I mean *really* free, and that made me feel very powerful."

"What do you mean when you say you felt powerful?"

"Like I said, it's hard to describe, but there's something about the kind of freedom you feel. You know, sex is a very possessive thing, and when you're having sex with more than one person, no one can possess you or think they're possessing you. Do you know what I mean?"

"Yes, I think I do," I replied. "But if it's all those good things, why don't you still do it?"

"That's the easiest question you've asked so far. Like I said before, it doesn't work with being a couple, probably because of what I was just saying—the possession thing. And I was in a couple for six years; we broke up just about a year ago. Anyway, that time's past. That's for when you're young and need to explore everything around you, not for this stage of life."

For the young and the not-so-young, however, this is the activity that ranks highest on most people's wish list, with well over half of those who have never tried it saying it's an active part of their fantasy life. "It's a big fantasy of mine, but I've never been in a position where I could make it happen," said 24-year-old John, a Phoenix electrician. "Some of my friends have done it, and mostly they say it was great. One of these days . . ." he concluded, laughing.

About a quarter of the study's population said they had experimented with some form of bondage, an activity more prominent in the under-35 groups than in the older one. Sometimes it was nothing more than one partner or the other being pinned down with hands over the head. "At times Judy's hands were over her head, and I'd grab her wrists and hold them down and she'd struggle a bit, but it was clearly an erotic turn-on for us," said 32-year-old Dan, a Denver salesman. "I've done it with other women, too, and I've always been surprised at what a turn-on it was for them. Sometimes if a woman is on top, she'll do the same to me. Obviously I'm strong enough to break her grip, and I'd play at trying to do it, and that only made it more exciting for both of us."

Sometimes people tied each other up, both men and women saying they enjoyed the dominance and submission side of the game equally well. "I can enjoy being tied up, and I like tying someone up," said 25-year-old Felicia, a New York editorial assistant. "It's part of the whole fantasy—sometimes to be the dominant one and then to turn it around into submission. The idea of being hurt or hurting doesn't interest me, but the idea of being dominated, or dominating someone, now that's interesting, and I've enjoyed acting it out sexually. It's all part of the theater of sex."

Then there are those who refuse to be bound in any way but who enjoy doing the binding. For them, the issue is always power and control. "I've been tied up, but I don't like it," said Steve, a 27-year-old New Haven restaurant manager. "But I sure like to tie a woman up. It's definitely a power thing. I think it's innate, maybe not only in the male but in human beings, to want to have sexual control over the partner. But in the male, the whole phallic thing represents power. It's something that extends out; it pushes; it penetrates. Everything about it says power and control. I used to play the electric guitar in a band, and the guitar became a phallic power thing. I'd take it and point it at women, and it was meant to be a gesture of sexual power. I've run into very few women who are turned off by that kind of thing, so I think it must be more common than people will admit."

But, in fact, there are women who are "turned off by that kind of thing," who insist that sexual excitement for them is in being in control. "I let someone tie me up once, only once and never again," said a 23-year-old Los Angeles typist adamantly. "It feels too, I don't know, too helpless and out of control. But I love to tie someone else up and have him in my power," she concluded, wringing her hands and making the face and voice of an old-time villain.

Most people of all ages gave a resounding "not interested" to other forms of sadomasochistic sexual activities, even in play. "Anything that even remotely suggests pain is absolutely not for me." "No, I wouldn't care for anything that might be painful." "Ugh! What could possibly be exciting about pain?" "Why would I want to hurt anyone or get hurt?"

The few who did engage in activities that involve giving or getting pain all insisted that they were "nothing serious," weren't really meant "to hurt someone." "It's just for fun. There's no bleeding or bruises or anything like that," said 25-year-old Jeff, a Washington government worker. "It's more like the art of teasing another person. There's sort of light pain involved, maybe not even pain but just getting to the edge of it, you know, where the next move would maybe hurt a little. It never was anything serious and certainly not dangerous."

"Can you say what it is about pain that turns you on?" I asked.

"I don't know; I ask myself that, too, but I don't know. It just feels good, more exciting, I guess you could say."

Why would pain feel good? The answer, I believe, lies in the early sexual history of the people for whom this is true. Several of the men and women who engage in these sadomasochistic activities told of having their first pleasurable sexual sensations when, as a small child, they were also being hurt. Sometimes it was during a spanking; other times it was at some kind of play. Whatever the source, in such instances pain and pleasure can become associated with each other, seeming almost as one, and sexual gratification comes to depend on the fusion of the two. Talking about how she had had her first orgasm on the seesaw in a neighborhood playground, 42-year-old Sheila, a Seattle secretary, explained, "I used to love the seesaw when I was a kid, and I'd sit on it for as long as they'd let me. I remember, I was maybe 5, my mother was on one end of it, and each time she'd let go, I'd come down with a bump. It was funny because it hurt, but it also felt good down there. I don't know exactly when, but after that, I'd try to re-create that good feeling. I'd find something hard, like the seat of my tricycle, and bounce up and down on it until the hurt and the good feelings came together. Of course, I didn't know I was having an orgasm then; it wasn't until much later that I realized what I was doing."

Several women who now find some measure of pain stimulating were the victims of sexual abuse in childhood. "From the time I was 9, my father was doing sexual things to me," recounted 34-year-old Faith, a social worker in Columbus. "He didn't actually penetrate me until later, on my twelfth birthday, but there were all kinds of things before then. I could kill him when I think about it now, but then, even though I was scared and he hurt me sometimes—especially when I was younger and he'd stick I don't know how many fingers inside me, or that first time, when he really did it—I have to admit, I got good feelings from it, too; I mean, real sexual feelings. As I got older, I would even come sometimes. I hated myself for it, and was ashamed, and all like that, but I have to admit it, it happened."

She paused, seemed to be lost in thought for a few moments, then continued with difficulty. "Dammit, that whole stinking business still affects me now. The only time I really get off sexually is with some guy who's totally unsuitable, even dangerous maybe, so that I'm kind of scared and ashamed of what I'm doing. And if there's some pain involved, not a lot, just a little, well . . . ," the words trailed off as her eyes swept the room. Then, picking up where she left off, "It feels good. I mean, I'm not a real freak who wants someone to really hurt me, but . . . I don't know; I don't think I can explain it," she concluded.

With sex so freely available now, I couldn't help but wonder: Who keeps prostitutes in business these days? And why? About one-fifth of the men I interviewed had made at least one visit to a prostitute. Some were young and looking for their first sexual experience. "I had my first intercourse with a prostitute at a brothel," said a 31-year-old Sacramento salesman, smiling in recollection. "I went with a group of guys; all of us had decided it was time. I imagine I was fairly fortunate. I had a nice lady. I tried to play it cool and didn't tell her it was my first time, but she must have known. She asked me what I wanted, but I didn't know what to say, so she started naming off things and what I could get for a certain amount of money. I said I had forty dollars and that I'd like her to do what would make me happy and what she'd enjoy, too. So I had half and half. She gave me some oral sex, then we had intercourse."

The rest were men, both single and married, who continued to see prostitutes periodically right through adulthood. For some of these men, a visit to a prostitute serves the same purpose it always has—a place to get something they can't get from the women in their lives. "Prostitution's a lot more important than most people let on," said 38-year-old Martin, a Baltimore lawyer. "It's something men aren't proud of, especially today when there's so much sex ready and waiting out there; so it's a big secret. But it's where those gaps in their relationships are filled."

"What about you? Do you go to prostitutes?"

"I haven't lately, but that doesn't mean I won't again. It's one of those things to do when what I really want isn't available, and I've made my share of treks to prostitutes."

"What do you mean when you say you want something that isn't available?"

"It can mean lots of things. Sometimes it's something a girl-friend—or when I was married, my wife—won't do, maybe like anal sex. But there's also times when it's a relief not to have to listen to somebody's directions about what she wants, and to be worrying all the time about her making it, too. It takes some of the pure physical pleasure away when you have to be thinking about somebody else. A prostitute doesn't want anything but to make you feel good. And it's better than masturbating because she's got a warm body," he concluded with a self-conscious laugh.

Some men say they seek out a prostitute when, as 32-year-old Jonathan, a Philadelphia public-relations man, put it, "I don't want anything that even resembles a relationship."

"You could get that at the bar around the corner," I remarked. "So what's the difference?"

"There's no possibility of rejection; it's a given; there's no effort. It's also totally single-minded. You know exactly why you're there. You do it and get on with it, and you don't have to worry about anything or anybody else."

Only three men had ever picked up a street prostitute, al-though others shamefacedly admitted they had fantasies of such an adventure. The massage parlors that now are available in most major cities of the country offer a more comfortable sub-stitute. In them, men can reduce the sense of shame and stigma attached to prostitution with the pretense that they've come for something else. "Sometimes I go to one of those massage parlors thinking that all I want is to get a massage and relax in the sauna," said 33-year-old Grant, an engineer from upstate New York, his gaze averted in discomfort as we talked. "But I have to admit, it never ends that way."

"Why would you go to a prostitute instead of to one of the

bars where you know you could meet someone to have sex with?"

"Because I want sex with no strings or anything else attached. I liken it to an elaborate health spa. You're getting showered down; you're in a sauna; and then there's sex. I sometimes find it very good for the soul. I would draw parallels to going to the gym and working out; it's working on a different part of your brain, that's all."

Sex "with no strings," sex that's "totally single-minded," sex that fills "the gaps in their relationships"—all probably at least some of the reasons why men have gone to prostitutes through the ages. But it seems to me there are other reasons as well, high among them the shifting power relations between men and women.

Along with the new sexual availability of women, which most men have greeted with pleasure, has come a new assertiveness— a shift that some men applaud, but that for others is a difficult challenge. It's not uncommon either for the same man to feel differently about it at different times—sometimes appreciating the change, sometimes wishing for a return to the acquiescence of the past. True, women have always had some control of the sexual interaction, even if only by developing the proverbial "headache" at bedtime. But generally their options were either to avoid sex or to submit passively. Now, they're much less likely to do either. Instead, they're more apt to be fully engaged in a sexual interaction and to expect their partner to attend to their sexual wishes and needs.

Consequently, men often talked about how women now make them "feel inadequate," how they're afraid they "can never do anything right," how they find it "impossible to satisfy some women these days." For some of those men, at least, a visit to a prostitute buys the illusion of power and control once again. He pays; she delivers on order. What else does it mean to talk about "sex that's single-minded," or to say "it's a relief not to have to listen to someone's directions"?

Beyond power, there's also sin. In an era when so little is proscribed, for some men at least, a visit to a prostitute may be connected to the excitement of the forbidden, to the sense that this is the one sin they can still commit. Although no one talked about this during the course of this research, I have worked with several such men in my years of practice as a psychotherapist. They were ordinary men, often professionals or executives, for whom the thrill of sex was connected to its illicit nature. As women became more available sexually, they found themselves in conflict. Intellectually, they appreciated the change; emotionally, they missed the forbidden and the sense of danger that had so heightened their sexual response. From time to time, therefore, they would seek out a prostitute, sometimes one who worked the streets, since there lay the greatest danger, therefore the most sexual excitement.

Although everyone in this study was self-defined as heterosexual, about one-tenth had some adult experience with members of the same sex, by far the largest proportion in the 18–34 age group. Given the intense homophobia evidenced by both adult men and teenage boys, it's no surprise that women were more likely than men to have experimented with same-sex relationships. I don't mean to suggest that straight women welcome lesbianism any more than men do male homosexuality. But not one woman or girl ever expressed the kind of virulent anger at the very thought of it that I heard so commonly from their male counterparts about gay men.

Partly, no doubt, the Gay Liberation Movement, which has forced us to attend to homosexuality in new ways, has made a difference in how straight and gay women relate to each other. But that can't be the whole answer, since the same movement has had far less impact on the homophobia of heterosexual men. Partly, also, the Women's Liberation Movement, which, after much struggle, brought lesbians and heterosexual women together in a common cause, can take some credit for women's greater ease in dealing with lesbianism. But while the importance of such movements in helping to change public consciousness is not to be denied, I believe there's a deeper-lying explanation as well, one that helps us to understand why these powerful social movements of our time influenced women so much more than men.

Once again, we start with the fact that, from infancy on, women have a long history of close and unbroken connection with each other. An emotional tie between any two women, therefore, is understandable to them, even seems natural. Moreover, since, as I already have said, the establishment of a sense of self and gender identity is direct and straightforward—a continuing integration of the primary identification with mother—women develop a strong and solidly internalized female identity. Consequently, although they may not understand the sexual attraction between two women, may even find it repugnant, the sight of a lesbian doesn't directly threaten their sense of self as woman.[4]

For a man, it's different. He has no history of deep and lasting emotional connections to other men that aren't complicated by fear and competition. Instead, from earliest childhood, a man, father, has been a competitor for the attention of a woman, mother. Good training for the competitive male world he'll face in adulthood, but not for his subsequent relations with other men, straight or gay. For most straight men, therefore, the idea of the kind of emotional relationship and vulnerability with another man that homosexuality implies is beyond comprehension.

Complicating the picture is the fact that homosexuality is equated with the feminine in this society and, as psychoanalyst Richard Isay has written, men have a compelling "fear and hatred of what is perceived as being 'feminine' in other men and in oneself."[5] We know, of course, that this dread and loathing is rooted in and reinforced by a society that denigrates the feminine and glorifies the masculine. But the origin of the fear, and the reason why it is so deeply embedded in male psychology, goes back to the need to renounce the early identification with mother in order to develop and consolidate a male gender identity. Since a man's male self is not defined directly by a primary identification with a male figure, but indirectly by the renunciation of the female, his sense of his maleness tends to be tenuous enough to require buttressing and protection against the reappearance of the repressed feminine side. As a man, therefore, he becomes anxious and fearful in the face of what he sees as the feminine

in another man—anxious about his own maleness, fearful of finding the despised feminine in himself once again, of opening up
the old dependencies he struggled to shut away so long ago.

Heterosexual male culture continues to reinforce this homophobia, of course. But I believe that its seeds lie in men's early
experiences with the feminine in mother and in themselves. By
understanding the impact of these developmental experiences
on later life, we can account for the persistence of men's revulsion
and hatred of homosexuality, even among those who would wish
they could feel otherwise.

The subject of homosexuality brings us to the tragedy of AIDS
and its effect on the sexual behavior of heterosexuals. Mention
the sexual revolution in a social setting, ask what happened to
it, and almost invariably someone will say, "That's easy, AIDS,"
while others nod in solemn agreement. That's the received wisdom. The reality, however, is quite another story.

It's true that AIDS is part of everyone's consciousness today,
that we think about it, talk about it, worry about it. Yet all this
has had relatively little bearing on what heterosexuals do about
it. Yes, there are some men and women who consistently refuse
to have sex with someone they don't know well without a condom. But even those people haven't stopped having sex. Yes,
many people now say they won't go to bed with someone they
meet for the first time. But by the second or third time, their
caution evaporates, even when they know little more about their
partner than they did on the first meeting. Yes, most people are
likely to be carrying condoms these days, but when the moment
of decision arrives, they often remain in wallet or purse. A study
of women's contraceptive practices from 1982 to 1987, years
when AIDS was headline news, found that the increase in condom use was negligible—from 12 percent to 16 percent.[6] And
the national Centers for Disease Control report that the incidence of all sexually transmitted diseases continues to increase
sharply, with the number of new cases of chlamydia exceeding
4 million in 1989 and the syphilis caseload reaching a 40-year
high and still climbing.

When it comes to practicing safe sex, most of the men and women I met were no different from those who make up these statistics. "Of course I worry about AIDS; it scares me to death," exclaimed 27-year-old Stacey, a TV producer in San Francisco, whose face clouded over with a troubled frown as she spoke.

"What do you do about it?"

"I never go out without condoms anymore. I have them right here," she replied, as she reached for her purse, opened it and pulled out the packet.

"And do you make certain they're used?"

She hesitated, looked uncomfortable, then with a dismissive gesture, "Well, I'm not as good about it as I should be, I know that. But they're such a pain. I don't like the way they feel, and men hate them, and it, well, it just spoils things. If it's somebody I really, really don't know—like a one-night stand, which I don't do very much anymore—then I make sure the guy uses it. But if it's someone where I think it could turn into some kind of a relationship or something, then I figure it's probably okay."

"So despite your fears, 'probably okay' is a risk you're willing to take?"

With a smile, "Well, I guess we all play the probabilities in something, don't we? No, that's not really how I want to answer you. I think at those times it just doesn't *feel* like a risk. Maybe I'm kidding myself, but you can only go by what things feel like. And, you know, when I think about it rationally, AIDS isn't much of a threat to someone like me, is it? I know all about what they're telling us. But how many straight people has anyone ever heard of with AIDS? I just don't think my risk of making love with someone who's a bisexual or an IV drug user is all that great."

By far most of the people in this study threw caution to the wind at least some of the time. Even some who said they took the threat seriously enough to get tested more often than not found themselves engaging in unprotected sex a short while later. "I've been tested, so I know I'm clean," said 28-year-old Morgan, a Chicago real-estate salesman. "But then I find myself in a position where I've just met some very pretty lady and I forget I don't have a condom with me, and pretty soon, well, it's just hard to stop when you get all worked up."

"What good does your test do, then?"

"Yeah, well, I've gotten I don't know how many tests, because afterwards I get worried," he replied, leaving his chair to walk around the room as he talked. "I tell myself I'm a dumb jerk, and I'm not going to do it again. But," with a sigh of resignation, as if it's all out of his control, "I don't know, maybe I'll drink too much or something. Also, when you're sitting with a group of people talking about AIDS, you think how frightening it is and that you'll never take a chance again. But then when you're right there face to face with this one person who's attractive and appealing, it's hard to see her as a problem or someone who's going to give you a death-dealing disease."

An interesting way to put it, isn't it? For it's hard, indeed, to imagine that someone who's so beguiling, someone with whom you want to engage in this life-giving activity we call sex, could threaten you with death. Equally important in the inconsistency between word and deed that's so common around AIDS are the words I heard spoken over and over again: "How many straight people has anyone ever heard of with AIDS?" A question that tells us that despite their stated fears it's hard to convince people that they're at risk when their personal experience violates the warning. And it is undeniably true that heterosexuals have continued to have unprotected sex with no visible untoward effect.

It's this dissonance between message and reality that enables people to live with the fear without significant alterations in their behavior. It's the same with any threat that seems to have no immediate reality in our lives—whether a dread disease or the possibility of war. We're aware of the possibility of catastrophe, experience the fear when, for whatever reason, it comes into awareness. But when anxiety rises, denial comes to the rescue— in this case aided and abetted by the fact that the threat and the lived experience are so much at odds.

In the abstract, then, people will speak of their fears and mean it. But as they live their lives, something else takes over. They meet an attractive person, one who's appealing aesthetically and sexually. They talk; they flirt; they laugh; perhaps they eat together. And dissonance enters, a sense of the incongruous. For the whole experience is totally at odds with the notion that somehow they're at risk, that this person who seems so connected to life, who stirs the life forces in them, could be the carrier of death.

I don't want to deny that AIDS has had a profound impact on our consciousness. For it is not irrelevant that we now know that sex can kill—knowledge that has changed our way of thinking about sex, even when it hasn't immediately transformed behavior. It's impossible to say with certainty what part the coming of AIDS has played in the shifts we have seen in sexual behavior. But in speaking with hundreds of people across the country, I found little evidence to suggest that AIDS has been much more than a catalyst, one that escalated changes already in process perhaps, but not the reason behind them. "The hysteria about AIDS was just a convenience so people could stop all that senseless fucking around," said Anne, a 36-year-old Milwaukee dance instructor, in a remark that was typical of the view people expressed.

It seems to me, then, that in this epidemic, stressful though it may be, heterosexual women and men have found an opportunity to stop what they already had tired of doing, to step back for a moment and try to redefine the dance of sex in ways that are more satisfactory to them. In the words of 37-year-old Scott: "Nothing happened to the sexual revolution; it's still going on. It just looks different now." Different, in this case, means that along with a much more open sexuality, people now talk also about wanting relationships of love and intimacy, commitment and constancy. But difficult issues remain to be resolved as we try to find our way to the kind of relationships we now say we want.

1. This is one of the areas in which there was a distinct class difference. Men from working-class backgrounds were more likely to want to hold women to more traditional sexual norms and less likely to feel a need to apologize for it.

2. Lillian Breslow Rubin, *Worlds of Pain: Life in the Working-Class Family* (New York: Basic/Harper Torchbook, 1976); see also Rubin, *Women of a Certain Age* (New York: Harper & Row, 1979).

3. A few women distinguished between what they called erotica and pornography. The former, they said, was usually European in origin and could be both interesting and stimulating, while the latter was characterized as exploitative and contemptible.

4. Carroll Smith-Rosenberg, *Disorderly Conduct: Visions of Gender in Victorian America* (New York: Oxford University Press, 1985).

5. Richard A. Isay, *Being Homosexual: Gay Men and Their Development* (New York: Farrar, Straus & Giroux, 1989), p. 78.

6. See Jacqueline D. Forrest and Richard B. Fordyce, "U.S. Women's Contraceptive Attitudes and Practice: How Have They Changed in the 1980s?" *Family Planning Perspectives* 20, 3 (May/June 1988): 112–118.

# 7

## The Quest
## for Relationships

Commitment and constancy! Strange words for these times, words whose meanings are shadowed by the reality that grown women and men continue to move in and out of relationships at will. Commitment and constancy! We speak the words easily, but they give us pause because we're no longer quite certain just what they mean, how we might achieve them or whether, in fact, we really want to.

Until recently, the road to commitment and constancy was clear. Marriage—a set of vows exchanged that are also a public statement of commitment, of willingness to assume responsibility for one another. Yes, it's a legal contract as well, but at the moment when people undertake it, the contractual element is the background music, the romantic "happily ever after" myth the foreground theme.

After three decades of rising divorce rates, we're far less certain. "I'd really like to get settled, but marriage, I don't know," said 34-year-old Mike, a computer programmer in Phoenix. "If

I had my choice I don't think I'd marry because I really don't believe in the institution anymore. It's been crippled, and people don't take it seriously, so why bother with it? I have so many friends who are married and cheat, and their wives cheat. No one respects what it means to enter into that union anymore. Sure, I want a long-term committed relationship with a family, but I don't see any reason to be a party to some meaningless ritual."

Is it just the reality of marriage as a troubled institution that underlies such words? Or is it also some fear of the tie that binds, some resistance to assuming the responsibilities and obligations that tie demands? Or are there other conflicts that make commitment difficult for so many people in these times?

In her book *The Hearts of Men*, Barbara Ehrenreich has written that men today are in "flight from commitment," that they are loath to trade the bachelor pad in the city for the house in the country, unwilling to give up their freewheeling, fun-filled lives for the burdens and responsibilities of marriage and children.[1] An analysis with which many women agree. "It's not like it was for the men in my father's generation," observed Lynne, a 33-year-old executive in Atlanta. "Men don't want to take on all that responsibility anymore. They don't want to have to worry about mortgages, and kids with runny noses, and all that stuff."

Undoubtedly this is true about some men, usually the more affluent managers and professionals who earn enough money to live the elegant lifestyle featured in films and magazines. But there's something wrong with the picture as drawn. First, it's a way of life most men in America cannot afford. Second, it leaves out all those who do marry and take on the "mortgages and kids with runny noses," often at considerable personal sacrifice. Third, it's precisely the men at the top who no longer have to meet those responsibilities by themselves, since they are most likely to be able to marry a professional woman whose earning capacity may not be far below, sometimes is even above, their own.

Certainly, as Ehrenreich argues, the media images are powerful influences in shaping our values and attitudes, and the fantasies they stir play a part in how we try to live our lives. But while men, like women, may dream of the glamorous life, most are all too aware of the difference between fantasy and reality. Just so, men may watch a Don Johnson or a Tom Cruise with visions of transformation dancing in their heads, but few delude themselves into thinking it's possible. For those who do become seduced by the dream and can afford to give it a try, it's usually a transient experience, part of the road to maturity, a stop on the way to real life. "For a few years it looked like heaven," said 36-year-old Paul, his brown-eyed gaze seeming to turn inward as he recalled those years. "I came out of law school and into this great job. I was working my ass off, but I was making a lot of money. I had no responsibilities, nobody telling me what I could do, my dream car—a Porsche 928—travel, all the women I wanted. Heaven! But it got old pretty fast. Now I'm ready to settle down, but finding the right woman to do it with . . . now, that's a problem."

The "problem," however, is not a dearth of appropriate women, but a surfeit of men's ambivalence about what they really want from a woman today.[2] In any revolution, those changes that benefit the dominant group will be realized most easily, while those that threaten their privileged position and the power that goes with it will be resisted most tenaciously. The sexual revolution, which brought large numbers of heretofore unavailable women into the sexual marketplace, was a great boon to men, a feast they probably couldn't even have dreamed of before. Therefore, the change was greeted eagerly. But the gender revolution, which called for the liberation of women from their traditional roles, threatened to disrupt the historic power relations between women and men, both in bed and out of it. *This* was another matter; *these* were demands to which men would not yield easily.

Thus, most men say they want a woman who's an equal, a social and intellectual companion, one who will share with them all the responsibilities of marriage and family life. Yet the very women who meet these qualifications also activate old tapes about appropriate role behavior, about femininity and masculinity. Consequently, men complain that women aren't "able to give to a relationship," that "they've lost the capacity for kindness," that "women don't know how to compromise anymore," that "there's such a thing as being too independent," that "women today don't want to be a wife, they want one," that "they've lost all balance between personal and professional life," that "too many women think compromise is surrender," that "women want it all now."

After hearing that last remark from several men in a row, I commented to Rob, a 28-year-old Reno blackjack dealer, "Perhaps you've forgotten that it's men who have had it all until now." Laughing, he replied, "Yeah, I hear that from women all the time, but who are you talking about? Maybe my father had it all, but I never have, and now I'm not even sure what a relationship's supposed to be about anymore."

This is no small matter for either women or men. The continuing changes in the definitions of femininity and masculinity, in the role expectations for woman and man, husband and wife, mother and father, have left everyone uneasy and uncertain. What is a good marriage today? How do the new man and new woman behave toward each other, toward the world? For the first time, the issue of balancing love and work does not belong to men alone. For the first time, it's no longer certain who will take care of home and hearth, relationship and children.

Most men deny their conflicts, insisting that women are to blame for the difficulties in relations between the sexes today. "I hate to say it, but women's lib has really screwed things. They pushed women to pursue their professional aspirations freely and, as a result, they're very confused about what role to play in their personal lives," said 40-year-old Owen, a Cleveland physician, the smile on his lips denying the anger in his eyes.

"I'm drawn to aggressive women who have careers because there's a certain energy a woman like that brings to life that I find very attractive," he continued after a short pause. "But unfortunately, women like that seem to have lost sight of who they are as women, or human beings, or people, call it whatever you want. All I know is that it's real hard to find a woman who's smart and hip and aggressive and who also can temper that with the needs of a relationship. And that screws up everything, including sexually."

"What would it mean to temper those things?"

"I mean she has to know how to be soft, you know, like a *real* woman."

But being "soft, like a real woman," doesn't quite do it either. "I want someone who's got some fire inside her and isn't going to be totally dependent on me," said a 32-year-old advertising manager in Chicago. "Some of the women I've met, they're so passive. Sexually, too, but that's not all I'm talking about. They want a great entertainer, someone who'll plan life for them. They're happy to get into all the activities you do and plan, but they don't bring enough to the party. I don't want to be the one putting all the energy and fire, not to mention money, into the relationship. It's important for me to be with someone who's willing and able to throw her share of logs on the fire." Pausing a moment to catch his breath and reflect, "So what I guess I'm saying is, I want a woman who can be a soul mate and a companion and my best friend; that's what I'm looking for."

"It seems to me there are plenty of independent women around these days, so why is it so hard to find what you want?"

"Yeah, well, I guess you have to watch out for the fact that men get scared of a woman who has her own bonfire and invites you to join her. They want it, but then they get kind of wary of a woman who can provide them with real entertainment and education and sensuality."

"You're talking about these abstract men. What about you?"

"Sure, sure, I mean me, too," he replied quickly, waving his hand as if to shake off the question. Then, as the silence lengthened between us, "Listen, it's not something I'm proud of, and I know it puts a real crimp into finding the woman I want to settle down with. When a guy realizes that a woman could be a real equal, or maybe even more than equal, it makes him nervous. When I'm with that kind of woman I have to combat the feelings of insecurity that come up, and there's the worry about being inadequate. So it's a bind. That's the type of woman

I want, but I have to admit, I also get jittery when I'm with
someone like that."

No matter what the class or ethnic group, among the never-
married men who are over 30, most talked about wanting to
settle down, and almost all said they wanted a woman who's
fully an equal partner in all areas of living. But equality has its
limits. And for most men, it falls by the wayside when they begin
to think about family responsibilities. "I want a woman who's a
real partner, and I have no problem with strong, aggressive
women," said 31-year-old Jason, a biochemist in Minneapolis.
"My mother is that kind of woman, and I've always admired her.
But one thing I know, when I get married, I want kids. That's
the real problem. Who's going to stay home and take care of
them? Somebody's got to raise them, and I don't want them
raised by strangers."

Most jobs don't allow the kind of flexibility that permits parents to share child rearing. Nor do they pay enough to permit
a family to live on less than two full-time incomes. But even
where flexibility would be possible and income sufficient, most
men still simply don't consider it their job. "What about you?
How would you contribute to raising the children?" I asked
Jason.

"I'm certainly willing to do all I can," he replied without
hesitation or defensiveness. "I don't expect to be an absent father, but someone has to take the larger share of responsibility.
Someone has to be home with them when they're very young,
or be there when they're sick or when they come home from
school later on. And I won't say I can do that, because I can't.
I have my career, and it's very important to me, what I've worked
for all my life."

Men, then, still take certain prerogatives unto themselves, as
if they were given in natural law, and women are left to deal
with messages that are wildly mixed. Be an equal, but not wholly
so. Be independent, but tread with care. Be assertive, but ready
to give way. Make money, but not too much. Commit to a career,
but be ready to stay home with the children. Be sexually aggressive, but don't push too hard.

Small wonder that so many women are angry and resentful. "These guys are oh so liberated, but it's all words, nothing but words," raged Liz, a 35-year-old Tucson architect. "Dammit, it makes me furious, because when it gets down to the brass tacks of real life, what they really want is a woman who can pay her share of the bills, then turns into some sweet little thing who looks up at them adoringly, cooks wonderful meals, takes care of the kids, and after all that, turns into a sexpot at midnight."

For the women over 35 who have never married or borne children, the bind can be excruciatingly painful. The biological clock keeps ticking and urgency grows. "Until now I've been cool about not being married or having kids, but now I'm beginning to feel it, that sense of desperation that I've heard other women talk about," said 37-year-old Abigail, a San Francisco executive, who pushed her dark bangs from her forehead agitatedly as she spoke.

Men, knowing this, are wary—a vigilance given further legitimacy by such recent hit films as *Fatal Attraction*, the bizarre story of a woman so desperate for a man that when he rejects her, she turns into a psychotic killer. "Maybe because I'm straight and successful, women seem very desperate," said 34-year-old Gary, a New York bond salesman. "There's no challenge. The women in their thirties, maybe they feel their days are numbered or something, but they behave like they have to hurry up and grab somebody before it's too late. It feels like they're strangling you to death. You get involved with one of those women and it feels like it has nothing to do with you as a person. It's only because I'm a man and fit the profile they're after."

Listening to such words spoken so often by men, it was hard to remember that there are plenty of women today who choose singlehood, women who live happy and comfortable lives in which loving friendships and satisfying work fill most of the corners. "I haven't seriously thought about marriage since I was a kid," said 39-year-old Suzanne, a professor in Texas. "I had to do some wrestling to decide if I was going to have a child by myself, but it wasn't the biggest trauma of my life when I decided not to do it. I have no objection to a man in my life; it's cozy when it happens. But I wouldn't want to live with anyone. It gets to be too much of a hassle, and you lose too much privacy and freedom."

But neither films, nor television, nor articles in the "Lifestyle" sections of the daily newspapers, nor stories in the weekly magazines chronicle the lives of such women. Partly that's because such stories are not nearly so dramatic as the sad tales of desperation wrought by the inexorable movement of the biological clock. But also, no doubt, because stories of women living successful single lives don't fit the mood of the moment, the nostalgia for a past when, myth has it, life was more predictable, relationships more stable, and women and men each happily enacted their roles in the family tableau.

Instead, we see the cautionary tales, stories that warn younger women to beware of their strivings for independence. An NBC White Paper documentary on single life, for example, shows high-level professional women in their mid to late thirties weeping on camera about the impoverishment of their lives, wondering aloud about their career choices because they remain unmarried and childless. Or a *Newsweek* cover story entitled "The Marriage Crunch" trumpets the findings of an unpublished demographic analysis by two social scientists in which they estimated that a 30-year-old single woman has only a 20 percent chance of marrying, while at age 35 the odds drop to 5 percent.[3] *Newsweek*'s writers failed to note, however, that, read another way, the same demographic data show that by age 40 over 90 percent of all American women will have married. Instead, they added their own interpretation to the data and speculated hysterically: "Forty-year-olds are more likely to be killed by a terrorist," and have only a 2.6 percent probability "of tying the knot." And just in case any woman might have missed the message, they concluded quite explicitly: "For many economically independent women, the consequences of their actions have begun to set in . . . Younger women will continue to face difficult choices about whether to marry and when. Chastened by the news that delaying equals forgoing, they just may want to give thought to the question sooner than later."

It's true, of course, that most women want to marry and have a family. But it's perverse to suggest, as these stories do, that those who can't find someone to share their lives are victims of their own strivings and to ignore the inequalities that still dominate the social-sexual relations between women and men. Yes, some women today are unwilling to enter a marriage that bears the mark of these inequities and compromises the lives they have built. But the problem lies not with the choice they have made but with the fact that they are still required to make it. Cynthia, a 36-year-old executive recruiter in Cincinnati, spoke eloquently about what marriage means to her now: "I think we've come full circle. When I was 13, all I ever thought about was getting married. By the time I was 20, the women's revolution had come along and I decided marriage was a prison, and it wasn't for me. Now that I'm 36, I know I want to get married, but only if I can have a relationship where there's some real equality—I mean a marriage that's a true intimate relationship where I don't feel like I'm in bondage."

Rather than having "come full circle," however, it seems to me that such women have drawn a new circle entirely. For the relationships they seek are far different from the ones their mothers entered willingly. The words they use to express their longings—marriage, home, children, family—may sound the same, but the images that underlie the words and give them their meaning are altogether different. They want marriage, yes, but a marriage that honors the life they have built—their work, their friends, their way of being in the world. They want home and family, yes, but not without intimacy, reciprocity and mutual responsibility for the welfare of all.

Partly because of such changes, we are left with difficult, seemingly intransigent, problems to resolve—large numbers of educated, accomplished women who can't find men with whom to share a family life within which their needs for intimacy, security and continuity will be met. Why, women will ask, can't men see the advantages to them in relationships that are more equitable, sexually and otherwise? They can, I believe. They gratefully accept the fact that they no longer have to fulfill the traditional male role alone. They're delighted with the sexual freedom of women that has given them so much pleasure, while it also has allowed them to explore their own sexuality in ways that were impossible before. They find excitement and challenge in women who can be real companions, who can meet them as social and intellectual peers.

But they see losses as well. In the private realm, they're not likely to find a woman like "dear old mom," a wife whose attentions are focused so heavily on her husband. And they've lost the right to sexual exclusivity that heartened "dear old dad." In the words of sociologist William Goode, they experience "a loss of centrality, a decline in the extent to which they are the center of attention."[4] In the public sphere, too, change means loss. They now must compete with women as well as men for the prizes they seek—for the status, prestige and money that, until recently, had been their rightful inheritance alone.

At the same time, their own lives aren't much improved. Most men still spend a lifetime working at the same dead-end, boring jobs they have always held, without any prospect of relief. True, their wives may be wage earners, too, these days, but the ultimate responsibility for housing and feeding the family generally still belongs to the men. It's they, not their wives, who are counted a failure when there's not enough money to pay the bills or to replace the children's outgrown shoes.

As their age-old bastions of privilege fall, men are caught in conflict, their sense of justice and fairness at war with self-interest. They feel resentment at the loss, even while they take advantage of the gains. They're angry at women, at the same time that they seek refuge in their arms. They try to enter the struggle to reshape their relationships, but their very identity, the only sense of self they know, feels under threat.

All this leaves men with the kind of ambivalence I have been speaking about. They want an achieving, assertive woman, while they also yearn for someone who will be sufficiently dependent

to enable them to feel safe, someone who will provide a protective and nurturant environment within which their needs and
desires will be met. They want a sexually exciting and responsive
woman at the same time that they wish for someone whose past
is not as colorful as their own, someone who, as one man said,
"isn't exactly a virgin, but whose experience is limited, yet she
knows how to be the perfect courtesan, like an inborn knowledge."

But it's not ambivalence alone that's at issue here. Power rears
its head as well—power in the form of what sociologist Arlie
Hochschild has called "backstage wealth," a term she uses to
refer to the support available to men and women as they pursue
their work outside the home.[5] Thus, for example, the wife who
irons her husband's shirts, cooks the family meals, stays home
from work when their child is ill, provides backstage support for
her husband's career. When such family tasks are not shared by
the husband, he is richer than she in the backstage wealth that
sustains life both at home and at work.

It's an evocative notion, applicable to other spheres of living
as well, as we try to understand the sources of power in relations
between women and men. As I use it here, backstage wealth
refers to the capital men and women are able to muster in their
interpersonal interactions. Such resources are "backstage" because they rest on cultural assumptions so firmly taken for
granted that they become part of the background of living, unseen and unacknowledged, therefore not up for modification and
negotiation. And it is precisely because of the inequality in backstage wealth each of us brings to the quest for relationships that
men can afford to nurture and nourish the conflicting voices
inside them.

The difference in what marriage and children mean to men
as compared with women gives men an advantage in backstage
wealth. So long as women are reared to find their identity in
marriage and motherhood, so long as this society enshrines
motherhood as the epitome of womanhood, marriage and children will assume a greater urgency for a woman than for a man.
It isn't that men want or need family life less than women. But

the fact that they are defined, and accordingly define themselves, as successful adults without it permits them to appear less needy, therefore in a position of greater strength and power than a woman.

Our social conceptions about youth, beauty and sexual desirability also are part of the inequities between us. We are a society that values a man for what he does in the world, a woman for how she looks. Consequently, a man of 50 is still in his prime, his years of experience, sexual and otherwise, a bonus in the relationship marketplace. But, for a woman, none of this counts. Instead, at 40 she's already over the hill. Like a fine wine, he gets better with age, but she deteriorates, wilting like a flower left too long in the sun. Translated into marriage statistics, this means that a divorced or widowed woman between the ages of 25 and 44 is only 65 percent as likely to remarry as a man in the same age group. For women between 45 and 64, the figure drops to 38 percent. For a man, that's backstage wealth, part of the negotiations between him and a woman, unspoken but understood by both to put her at a distinct disadvantage in the quest for a relationship.

Finally, the biological differences between men and women help to further distort the already existing power imbalance between them. For a woman in her thirties who wants to have children, the ticking of the biological clock puts her under pressure for a relationship that's unknown to a man.

All this notwithstanding, men are not the only ones who are caught in conflict. Women, too, are ambivalent about marriage and are conflicted about what they want in their relationships with men. The same women who talk about wanting to marry also worry about what it will cost. "I didn't want to get married when I was younger because I had to prove I could do it on my own," said 37-year-old Laura, a bank loan officer in Atlanta. Then, surveying her office with her eyes and a sweep of her hand, she continued proudly: "I've done that now, and for the last three or four years I've actively been looking for the right guy. I really want to get married and have children very much now, but the men I meet are scared as hell of making that kind of a commitment."

"Do you mean you haven't met one man in these years who isn't frightened of marriage?"

Hesitating for a moment, then, "I guess if I'm absolutely honest, I can't say that. But when it gets right down to it, maybe I get a little scared myself. I mean, I *do* want to get married, but I look at some of my married friends, especially when they have children, and it's no picnic. It doesn't seem like much of a life, and I begin to wonder whether I'm cut out for that. Some of my friends are talking about giving up their careers and staying home with the children, but I know I could never do that. I swore I'd never be dependent on anyone and live the life my mother lived, and I never will." Words that echo in the hearts of many women and keep them from marrying just as surely as men's conflicts do the same.

To speak of the conflict women suffer should not distract us from the lived experience on which their ambivalence rests. So long as the balance of power favors men, the gendered division of labor in the family will persist, and most women will bear a disproportionate share of work in the home, even when they are also fully employed outside it. In fact, studies show that, despite the fact that men have increased their participation in the household dramatically over the last two decades, women still spend twice as much time as men in household tasks.[6]

For poor and working-class women—those who work at low-paying, dull, routine jobs with nothing to look forward to—even such an inegalitarian marriage may offer the possibility of a better life than they can have alone. But women in the upper echelons—the managers and professionals who do satisfying work and also earn good money—have the social and economic resources to choose not to marry and still create a life that fills many of their needs. It's not ideal to be sure, since the yearning for an intimate love relationship is not easily stilled. But for some women, at least, it's better than the compromises they fear they'll have to make.

The inequality in marital roles is not the only issue that foments women's ambivalence, however. For, like men, they have their own version of wanting the impossible. Men want an assertive, successful woman who will be happy to stay home and care for the children. And women want a tender, sensitive, gentle man who's also the head of a Fortune 500 company. "I know it's not the way I'm supposed to feel," apologized 32-year-old Holly, a successful investment broker in Syracuse. "But I can't imagine being married to a man who's not at least as ambitious and successful as I am."

"Yet you used the words 'sensitive' and 'feeling' to describe the man you're looking for. Doesn't that seem contradictory to you?"

"Maybe," she retorted quickly, "but because I want a guy who's sensitive doesn't mean I want a wimp."

"Are you saying any man who's less successful than you are is a wimp?"

Looking uncomfortable, but shaking her head vigorously, "Well, no, not exactly. But a lot of these guys who don't have any real drive *are* wimps. I mean, you still want a man to be a *man*, don't you?"

"Wimp"—a word women use often to describe men who seem to them to be passive and dependent, a characterization about which men complain bitterly. "It really pisses me off," exploded a 30-year-old engineer in Detroit. "These women are always talking about how they want a man who's different, you know, one who's not just an aggressive prick. Then when a guy tries to be like that, what happens? They call him a wimp."

These are difficult binds for both of them, the products of a changing culture in which neither is certain anymore what to expect or want of the other. For the roles we have all been taught for so long, and the values they embody, die hard. It isn't that men don't mean it when they say they want a more aggressive woman, or that women are lying when they say they want a more sensitive man. But they can't give up wanting the other side as well. So he wants the "perfect courtesan" with "inborn knowledge"; she, the man who, as one woman said, is "a shark at work, a pussycat at home." He wants a woman who can "throw her share of logs on the fire," but he needs reassurance that he can control the fire. She wants "a man to be a *man*," while she also craves the kind of nurturance and sharing she gets from a woman friend. It's this ambivalence that disables some women and men from making the kind of commitments they seek. It's these conflicting desires they will have to reconcile if they are to live in the relationships they now say they want.

Sexually, too, ambivalence rears its head in this quest for relationships. After years of experience with relationships that never grew much beyond the sexual connection, many people now wonder whether it's better to wait until they know each other better, until they have established some basis besides sex for moving ahead. "When you jump into bed like that, I think things just get stuck there," explained 35-year-old Brad, a New Jersey salesman, his chin resting in his hand as he spoke. "I mean, there was probably no reason to get into bed in the first place; I mean, no reason besides sex. But once you do it, you get involved, maybe because it's easy, or you're lonely, or . . . I don't know what. Then, after a while, you know this isn't for you, so you have to get out and start all over again. What a pain!"

"So why do you keep doing it that way?" I asked.

He laughed, looked heavenward as if to search for the answer there, then replied, "I don't know; I keep asking myself the same question. It's confusing; you sort of know what's right, but you can't pull it off."

Repeatedly, both women and men spoke of this dilemma, some telling of the promises they make to themselves which they soon find they can't fulfill. "I think maybe when you get into sex so quickly you miss out on exploring other parts of the relationship and its possibilities," said Gail, a 36-year-old social worker from Philadelphia. "Personally, I've come to the conclusion that you shouldn't go to bed with someone until you've known him for a few months."

"Is that what you do now?" I asked.

"Well, not exactly," she replied, sighing as she spoke. "I keep

saying I will, but I don't know what happens. It's just hard to
hold out."

"Is that because the men put pressure on?"

She thought for a moment, then replied, "No, I don't think
so. I've dated men who said the same thing, and we agreed right
at the beginning that we'd wait until we saw whether something
was really there. But then, a week or two later, it just seems
like you can't do it, that's all. I mean, you've seen each other a
couple of times, and you like each other and feel turned on, and
. . . Well, there just doesn't seem to be any reason to wait. It
feels like a meaningless exercise in suffering or self-deprivation
or something like that."

A little more than two decades ago, deferring sexual gratification was the norm; now it's a "meaningless exercise in suffering
or self-deprivation." Why? What goes on inside these women
and men that makes it so difficult to put sex on hold, even when
they think it would be in their own best interest?

The answer, I think, is that a profoundly changed sexual consciousness lives inside these children of the sexual revolution, a
new consciousness that doesn't include deferring sexual gratification—at least not for very long—any more than it lets them
put off eating for days when they are hungry. Such change in
consciousness, however, cannot have taken place without a con-
comitant transformation in the very structure of desire itself, in
when and how desire is activated, experienced and acted upon.
These, it seems to me, are among the most significant changes
wrought by the sexual revolution, the ones whose effects will
prove to be most lasting. And these, also, are the ones so many
people now struggle with as they try to make sense and order
out of their own sexual behavior.

Important as the issues I've been discussing are, they are not
the only barriers to finding the relationships people want and
need. For along with the sexual and gender revolutions, we have,
in these last decades, been witness also to a new dimension in
the therapeutic revolution that has been with us since Freud's
work reached our shores.

By the time World War I was upon us, Freudian theory had

made its mark on American intellectual thought. The idea of the unconscious in mental life drew thinkers and writers like a magnet, and notions of sublimation and repression, especially in the area of sexuality, were quickly popularized. But Freud's dour view of the catastrophic consequences of a human nature left unchecked never fit well with American optimism and the individualist philosophy that undergirds all aspects of the nation's life.[7] The belief in the perfectibility of humankind, whether in personal or institutional life; the conviction that happiness would be ours if only we could find the right path—these are the ideas on which this nation was founded. They would not succumb lightly to an alien pessimism, even in the face of such human tragedy as the events of World War II.

Soon, therefore, psychologists were refashioning and redefining Freudian doctrine into a vision more suited to the American temperament, into theories that offered a more hopeful ("humanistic," some called it) view of human nature and its possibilities. During the 1960s, that decade when everything seemed possible, a variety of humanistic and existential psychologies emerged, all critical of the Freudian view that psychoanalysis can promise only to replace the pain of crippling neurosis with the unhappiness of everyday life. Instead, these new theories, dressed up in the language of continued development into adulthood and beyond, rested on older ideas of human perfectibility.[8] With this as their starting point, it was a small step to propose the possibility of unlimited personal growth and to urge upon all the quest for "self-actualization." The route to the goal was to be "self-awareness," a state, they promised, that was within the grasp of all.

It's no surprise that these ideas found immediate resonance among so many Americans. They were, after all, grounded in social changes that had been in process for most of the century. The continuing shift from rural to urban life, the growth of a strong, educated middle class, the increasing isolation of the nuclear family, the steady movement from a production to a consumer society, the explosion in communication technology that brought new ideas about self and relationships into homes across the land—all these were the social changes out of which a new dimension in American culture was being forged. All these already were calling for changing definitions of self, new conceptions of relationships, enlarged expectations of the possibilities in life. What was different about the sixties and seventies was the emergence of a systematic body of psychological thought that gave legitimacy to these new aspirations.

Whatever the original intent of this Human Potential Movement, as these new therapies soon became known, reasonable ideas of self-awareness and self-actualization soon became corrupted by a narcissistic involvement with self and a feverish search for instant gratification.[9] Encounter groups, the offspring of Gestalt therapy, swept the land. In them, people were assured that they could experience instant intimacy if they would only follow the rules to live in "the here and now," to get "in touch" with their feelings and express them "in the moment." Fritz Perls, father of Gestalt therapy, formulated the Gestalt prayer: "I do my thing, and you do your thing. I am not in this world to live up to your expectations. And you are not in this world to live up to mine."[10] "Do your own thing!" became the slogan of the age. The Me decade of the seventies was born.

But paradox haunted the therapeutic revolution just as it confounded the sexual revolution. The same movement that talked about happiness and encouraged the search for a quick fix also insisted on the need for "struggle" in relationships. The same theories that promised instant gratification also gave us the sober "no pain, no gain." Relationships don't just happen, we were told. They require work, hard work, without guarantee of reward.

Playfulness? Fun? These are alien words in the realm of relationships. "You have to work at it," we tell each other somberly, as we hasten off to the nearest couples therapist in search of some relief from our conflicts. So hard do we "work at it," in fact, that in some of the more affluent sectors of society, it's not uncommon for a couple to have three therapists: his, hers and theirs. But just what we're working toward, what we're looking for, often remains elusive, a mystery we can't seem to solve.

It's no surprise, then, that the idea of a lifetime commitment frightens not just men but women as well. Indeed, this may be one of those times when men's more obvious ambivalence serves to mask the conflict so many women also feel. "It scares me to death, the idea of being locked into a relationship that has lost its energy and meaning and that isn't vital and growing," said 31-year-old Jessica, the owner of a small business in Seattle. "But on the other hand, I begin to feel the fear of getting older and being alone, and I think about wanting some continuity and someone who means something to me to be there." She stopped, then with a short laugh that was almost an expletive, "I guess I want you to tell me it's possible, but even if you could, I wouldn't believe you, so what difference does it make?"

Our fantasy of achieving perfection, whether in self or other, consigns us to the search for the perfect relationship. "Every time I've met a woman I thought I could marry, I've been haunted by the idea that there's another one out there I might miss, you know, someone who's better or smarter or more beautiful or sexier, the woman of my dreams who's just perfect," said 41-year-old Carl, a Boston engineer. "But I'm past 40, and I begin to wonder: What the hell am I doing to my life? God, what a lousy mess we've gotten ourselves into. I love kids; I want a family. How long can I keep looking?" he asked, his words coming easily, but the pain on his face reflecting his loneliness and, somewhere inside him, the knowledge that his was an impossible dream.

This is the social and psychological framework within which our quest for relationships has gone on until now. Theoretically, these new psychologies held out the promise that our relationships would be better, more fulfilling, even more lasting, if each of us brought to them a fully mature, actualized self. The explorations in sensuality and sexuality, the "touchie-feelie" encounter groups, promised the possibility of a more open, more emotionally toned, guilt-free sex. Actually, relationships, sexual and otherwise, fell victim to the surging preoccupation with self. For there was a contradiction built into the theory. To become a couple, to be able to commit to being "we," means we must be willing to give over some part of the "I"—a need that soon comes into conflict with the quest for personal gratification and self-actualization. For sex to be wholly satisfying, we must have at least as much concern for a partner as for self—a requirement that doesn't live comfortably alongside the exhortation to "do your own thing." In the end, we are left with an extraordinarily heightened set of expectations about the possibilities in human relationships that lives side by side with disillusion that, for many, borders on despair.

1. See Barbara Ehrenreich, *The Hearts of Men* (Garden City, N.Y.: Anchor Press/Doubleday, 1983).
2. For a study of college students, which shows that they express conflicts similar to those described by the men I met, see Mirra Komarovsky, *Dilemmas of Masculinity* (New York: W. W. Norton, 1976).
3. June 2, 1986.
4. William J. Goode, "Why Men Resist," *Dissent*, Spring 1980.
5. Arlie Hochschild, *The Second Shift: Working Parents and the Revolution at Home* (New York: Viking Press, 1989).
6. John P. Robinson, "Who's Doing the Housework?" *American Demographics*, December 1988: 24–28, 63, and Hochschild, *The Second Shift*.
7. See Sigmund Freud, *Civilization and Its Discontents* (New York: W. W. Norton, 1961), for an extraordinarily powerful statement about the human potential for destruction—a vision born of his conceptualization of the individual as a mass of id impulses which society must keep in check until its norms are internalized in the form of the superego.
8. See, for example, Eric Berne, *Transactional Analysis* (New York: Grove Press, 1961); Abraham Maslow, *Toward a Psychology of Being* (New York: Van Nostrand, 1962) and *The Farther Reaches of Human Nature* (New York: Viking Press, 1971); Rollo May, *Existential Psychology* (New York: Random House, 1961) and *Love and Will* (New York: W. W. Norton, 1969); Frederick S. Perls, *Gestalt Therapy Verbatim* (New York: Bantam Books, 1971); Carl Rogers, *On Becoming a Person* (Boston: Houghton Mifflin, 1961); A. J. Sutich and M. A. Vich, *Readings in Humanistic Psychology* (New York: Free Press, 1969).
9. For some interesting critiques of this era, see Christopher Lasch, *The Culture of Narcissism* (New York: W. W. Norton, 1979) and *The Minimal Self* (New York: W. W. Norton, 1984).
10. Perls, *Gestalt Therapy Verbatim*.

# 8

---◆·◆---

# Sex and
# the Coupled Life

*F*or generations of the past, marriage typically meant a whole series of beginnings, not least among them sharing bed and breakfast with a loved one of the opposite sex. Most men probably had some experience with sexual intercourse before marriage, but rarely with a "good" woman. For women, it usually meant the initiation into an adult sexual relationship. Even for those relatively few whose explorations during courtship included sexual intercourse, there was an extraordinary difference between the guilty, if passionate, tumblings in the back seat of a car, the corner of a park or the living-room couch and the luxury of a bed of their own, unconstrained by concerns about time or parents.

For them, then, marriage meant the opening up of a whole new way of life. There were problems, to be sure. Not just women but men, too, were likely to be ignorant of anything beyond the rudiments of sex. Even if they knew something about it, most people had no experience in communicating about sex, and few even had a language with which to do it. Women, whose sexuality had been repressed for so long, found they couldn't become sexual libertines at the pronouncement of the marriage vows. Still, for the first time, sex came out of its shameful hiding place to become a part of everyday life.

But for the post–sexual revolution generations, marriage usually follows a period of sexual exploration with a variety of partners and is as likely to be a continuation of an already existing household as the beginning of a new one. Even when couples marry without having lived together, the full range of sexual experience will almost surely be thoroughly familiar to them when they find themselves in the marriage bed. Rarely, therefore, do they go through the period of sexual apprenticeship that preoccupied so much of the early weeks and months of marriage in the past. Instead, they come to marriage with a sexual relationship already blossoming, a good deal of experience behind them and a vastly increased set of expectations of sexual pleasure in the time ahead.

Paradoxically, the very experiences that ease their way also can create their own difficulties and disappointments as sex in marriage is compared with the variety and excitement of the period before. "Things change when you get married; the whole sex thing changes," said 35-year-old Randy, a Sacramento carpenter, married four years. "I figure it must have been easier to adjust to that when people didn't have so much experience to compare it to. If you don't know what you're missing, maybe you're better off."

Researchers into marriage and family life have found repeatedly that each member of a family writes its biography differently, and that husbands and wives often have what one prominent sociologist has called "his and her marriage"[1]—one marriage, two different stories to tell. The couples in this book were no different, not infrequently sounding as if they had two different sex lives, each convinced her or his version was the real one.

So, for example, there was considerable disagreement about the frequency of sexual activity and about the amount of time spent at it. Almost always the partner who wished for more had lower estimates than the one who did not. When they both were relatively well satisfied with their sex life, the disagreements were not large. A wife who said their sex life was "excellent," but still wished it was "a little more frequent," reported that, on the average, they had sex about six times a month. Her husband, who had no complaints at all, thought it was "eight or nine times." As the imbalance in the frequency of desire grows, so does the disparity in their reports. A husband who was actively dissatisfied said they had sex "once a week, sometimes less." His wife, who resented his sexual demands, said they get together "at least twice, sometimes three times a week." He said they "give it plenty of time, maybe forty-five minutes, sometimes more." As she told it, "it's usually quick, too quick—fifteen, maybe twenty minutes at most."

Despite such differences, the trend in the data is unequivocal. Sexual interest and activity are at their height during dating and courtship, take a drop when people begin to live together, then another fall after marriage, and show the most precipitous decline after the first child is born. It may be more or less dramatic, more or less troublesome to the particular individuals involved, but the patterning of the response is undeniable.

What happens?

Time and pressure—these are the answers most people give as they struggle to understand where the excitement and passion that first brought them together has gone. Time and pressure—problems that are pervasive and important enough to warrant a *Time* magazine cover story. Entitled "How America Has Run Out of Time," the article proclaims: "Workers are weary, parents are frantic and even children haven't a moment to spare: leisure could be to the '90s what money was to the '80s."[2] For the average American, the article tells us, free time has shrunk 37 percent since 1973, while the workweek, including commuting time, has increased from 41 to 47 hours. And that, of course, doesn't count many of the professions where 60-hour workweeks are standard and 70–80 hours not uncommon.

These are pressing problems, to be sure, problems that create

difficulties in every facet of family life. Yet, without denying
their reality, time and pressure alone cannot account for the
decline in both frequency and intensity in the sex lives of so
many couples. Otherwise, how do we explain the fact that the
same couples found time for a very active sex life before they
were married? They had the same jobs, lived with the same
daily pressures and, in addition, probably had to travel across
town to see each other after the day's work was done. "I don't
know what happened; it worries me a lot," said a 26-year-old
office manager from Tacoma, her eyes brimming with unshed
tears. "It's all changed so much in the two years since we've
been married."

"Could you say what's changed?"

Gesturing impatiently, "Everything, just about everything.
When we were dating and in love and in the throes of passion,
nothing was ever routine. We made love, we didn't just have
sex. There was this intense interest in each other, in exploring
each other's body. We were busy then, too, maybe even worse,
but we were *never* too tired or too busy. We'd meet for lunch
sometimes and never get back to the office because we went
home to bed and stayed there for the rest of the day. I still meet
him for lunch sometimes, but nothing like that ever happens
anymore."

"How do you account for such dramatic changes?"

"I've been thinking about it a lot for the last couple of months,
and I don't know; I just don't know. There's never time just to
relax and enjoy each other; there's so much pressure all the
time."

What happens?

External pressures come together with internal psychological
ones to take their toll. Sometimes the external pressures stimulate or create the internal ones. People begin to feel that their
very selves get dissolved, lost in the pressures of daily life. Under
such circumstances, the pleasure of sex can disappear, replaced
by the threat to the integrity of the self. At other times the
internal strains have a life of their own, born of anxieties and

fears that may be excited by the present situation but have their origin in earlier times and relationships.

On the most mundane level, the constant negotiation about everyday tasks leaves people harassed, weary, irritated and feeling more like traffic cops than lovers. Who's going to do the shopping, pay the bills, take care of the laundry, wash the dishes, take out the garbage, clean the bathroom, get the washing machine fixed, decide what to eat for dinner, return the phone calls from friends and parents? When there are children, the demands, complications and exhaustion increase exponentially. And hovering above it all are the financial concerns that beset most families in the nation today.

Under these conditions, some couples find themselves locked in anger—sometimes acknowledged, often not. As the tasks of maintaining life inside the family fall more heavily on the wife, she feels exploited. "How can I feel sexy when I feel so damned harassed and used? When I come home from work after he's been there for maybe an hour or more and the house looks like a disaster area, I could kill him, not screw him. If he'd make some effort to be more of a partner, I'd be a lot more loving." As she withdraws, his disappointment gives rise to a gnawing resentment, which makes it easier for him to justify his behavior, but is no help at all for their ailing sex life. "She says if I'd help out around here more, we'd have a better sex life. But that's just her excuse. She's always got one, no matter what I do."

Even where relative harmony reigns, the almost endless series of tasks, demands, needs unfilled do nothing to foster the kind of romantic feelings that tend to stimulate sexual desire. "Christ, by the time we get through dealing with all the shit of living, who cares about sex? I sometimes think it's a miracle that we still want to do it at all," said 28-year-old Brian, a Detroit factory worker, married nine years, the father of two small children.

Some couples seemed to have no problems with the change in their sex lives, explaining that passion remained high, even though things "look different." Usually this meant their preoccupation with sex had diminished and frequency had declined, a fact that seemed to bring them a certain amount of relief since, as 30-year-old Kevin said, "We don't have to be thinking about it all the time and can put our energy and thoughts into other places."

Others saw the change in their sexual activity as part of the normal pattern of living, something to be expected once a relationship becomes fully stabilized. And while they viewed this with some regret, it wasn't in the forefront of the issues that concerned them. "I think sex sort of had to change after we began living together," said 34-year-old Allen, an Indianapolis dentist in a four-year marriage with no children. "It started out on such a high pitch, it was a little too hot to handle at the beginning. Also we both work a little too hard, more than is good for either of us, so there's a lot of pressure and not much time. It's a rather arduous lifestyle, but it's what we both want to do, so it's something you accept. It's pay as you go."

His wife, 29-year-old Laurie, a nurse, regretfully agrees and also talks about the ways in which they try to compensate. "When we first met sex was much wilder, much more acrobatic, a lot of energy and lasted for hours, and much more frequent. Now it's rare when it's as open-ended and wild as it was in the early days. But occasionally, maybe once a month, we set aside an afternoon, and then we can still make it happen. Maybe I'd like to have more sex, more frequency, more activity, but overall I think it works out fine."

In their heads, most couples agree with Allen and Laurie. But their hearts tell another story. They may acknowledge that the sexual connection in marriage embodies new levels of comfort, companionship, safety and intimacy—qualities they value highly. But they also mourn the passing of the intensity, passion and frequency that were formerly theirs and long for the excitement and wonder sex once brought to their lives. "Sherry and I have a great thing going, and we both know that sex is only a part of a relationship," said a 32-year-old Detroit car salesman, married seven years with one child. "I don't want you to misunderstand me; I'm not unhappy with our sex life, and I think Sherry's the greatest. But I get to miss all that passionate excitement we used to have. Now, it's something we do, and I enjoy it a lot, but it's different. It feels like something's missing. Once in a while something happens—I don't know what—and you get a little taste of it again, and you wonder: Why can't we make this happen all the time?"

"Is there something that replaces the intensity and passion?"

"Sure," he said after a reflective pause, "but it's hard to find the words for it. When you know each other like we do now, it's different, easier, I guess you could say. I don't want to sound like a cornball or anything, but the way we love each other is deeper, and I guess the sex is, too." He stopped talking and looked away for a moment, then continued, "Christ, I said it, but I'm not sure I know what I mean. What the hell does 'deeper' mean? I know I feel something different, but I don't know if it's deeper or what. All I know is something's gone, and I don't know if that's the way it's supposed to be, or if there's something else we should be doing, or what. Maybe I'm just repeating what I hear all the time. There's so much crap out there all the time about sex, you don't know what to think."

"You don't know what to think"—one of the problems that baffle couples as they struggle with the changes in sex that come with living together in long-term committed relationships. For with all the talk about sex, we know little about the sexual behavior of real people, living real lives with all the social and psychological pressures that attend them.

Who knows what happens in the bedroom of even best friends? "We're very close to this other family; we've even gone away on vacation together a couple of times. But sex is the one thing we never talk about. Oh, there's some kidding around about it sometimes, but never anything serious so you'd get to know about each other's sex lives," said 26-year-old Joanne, a Richmond housewife, married six years with two children.

For most of us, knowledge about what people do, how often they do it or how they feel about it is conditioned by the images in the popular culture and the books we read, not by the experiences of others like ourselves. "You see all this stuff about sex all around, and you begin to feel like if you're not tearing your clothes off in the back seat of a limousine, like Kevin Cost-ner and what's-her-name, you're missing the real thing," Joanne continued.

Couples talk often about searching for creative ways to in-crease sexual interest and passion. Some manage to find them at least part of the time. For them, the loss is not so keenly felt. They tell of trying different positions and different places. "When you have kids, they make a real impact on your sex life," said 31-year-old Tony, a Seattle public-health official, married eight years with two children. "But we keep trying, experi-menting with different positions and things like that. If we're sure the kids are asleep, sometimes we'll do it on the living-room floor, but that has to be quick because you never know. And once a month we send the kids out to a babysitter and have dinner out, and then have the rest of the night at home in bed all by ourselves. It's one of the ways you compensate for having kids around; they take such a hell of a lot from you," he concluded with a sigh.

Others tell of using fantasy and of finding ways to meet at times other than the usual one. "We tell each other our fantasies, then try to act them out," said 38-year-old Martin, a salesman from suburban New York, married eleven years with two chil-dren. "We also use whatever opportunity we have to make sex a little different. I'll try to get off and come home in the middle of the day sometimes, or she'll wake me in the middle of the night. So maybe we don't do it as often as before, but the variety helps keep the excitement up."

But for reasons they don't understand, many couples find it hard to sustain such attempts to enliven their sex lives. "It's hard; we try," said Marian, a 26-year-old cashier, married five years with two children. "He's asked that we do different kinds of things, and we try. But when it comes down to it, it doesn't always work. If I put on sexy underwear, sometimes it works, but other times he's too tired, and I don't care a lot anyway," she concluded dispiritedly.

Even when people tell of successful attempts to stimulate sexual excitement and desire, they don't necessarily become

integrated into their lives. "We plan a romantic evening sometimes—light the fire, candlelight, good wine, the works," said
37-year-old Philip, an insurance broker from Charleston, married twelve years with two children. "It's great when we do it;
we can get really turned on. You know, I think sex begets sex,
because we'll do it more often for a week or so afterwards."

But somehow the experience isn't repeated. "When we do it
and it feels so good, we promise each other we'll do more things
like that, but we get busy with the crap of living—work, kids,
chores, balancing the damn checkbook—and we just don't get
around to it again."

What happens?

Sometimes the reasons for the waning of sex after marriage
are relatively easily traceable. In about one-fourth of the couples,
for example, sex was the battleground on which other, more
serious conflicts were played out. A woman who learns her partner has had an affair suddenly becomes uninterested in sex. "It's
hard to get into it; I'm just so tired all the time lately."

A husband who resents his wife's taking a promotion that
requires some travel suddenly begins to have erectile problems.
"It never happened until recently, but now, all of a sudden, I'll
go soft right in the middle of things."

Another who experiences his wife as a critical presence in his
life refuses to have sex for months on end, no matter what
enticements she offers. "I don't feel like it. What can I say?"

A wife who says, "My husband never talks to me," suffers
from migraines, which usually come on in the evening. "The
doctor can't figure out why they happen so much at night. He
thinks it might be some kind of night allergy."

A husband who complains that "sex has become a calendar
event" falls asleep at the appointed time. "I get tired, and right
away she's got a whole story about it."

A wife who's angry because her husband travels a great deal
and leaves her with full responsibility for their two children gets
herpes outbreaks when he's home far more often than when he's
gone. "It's a real problem. He's not home that much, and half
the time, maybe more, I've got a herpes attack."

A husband who competed with another man for years for the woman who's now his wife becomes an inattentive and disinterested lover soon after the marriage. "We have sex maybe once every two months or so. He just seemed to lose interest after we got married. Before that, he was by far number one in the lover category, all the things a woman would want, sensitive, passionate—really far and away the best lover I've ever had."

But there are other, less dramatic reasons as well. Everyone knows that good sex can cement a relationship. During courtship, therefore, when there's pressure to "catch" the other, both men and women may put on a great sexual act—the man being extraordinarily attentive to the woman's needs, the woman having ecstatic orgasmic experiences. Once married, the chase is over; the conquest made; the act no longer necessary. "When we first met, I thought we had this fabulous sex life," recalled 35-year-old David, an Atlanta commercial artist, who had been married for five years and divorced for one. "I thought she was the most sexually responsive woman I'd ever known. Then, after we were married she was, I don't know, she was never quite satisfied and always complaining about our sex life. I couldn't figure out what happened; then a couple of years later I come to find out the whole thing was an act. She told me she'd been faking it all along. I couldn't believe it! I could have killed her."

"Did she ever say why she did it?"

His elbows on the table in front of him, head in hands, voice weary, he spoke into the tabletop. "Yeah, she admitted that she'd have done anything to attract me and get me."

Often, however, the changes in sexual frequency and intensity stem from issues that are more subtle, more difficult to see. Freud wrote long ago: "It can easily be shown that the psychical value of erotic needs is reduced as soon as their satisfaction becomes easy. An obstacle is required in order to heighten libido; and where natural resistances to satisfaction have not been sufficient, men have at all times erected conventional ones so as to be able to enjoy love."[3]

Once we enter a long-term committed relationship, the barriers fall. There's nothing left to climb over, nothing to conquer.

Nancy, a 25-year-old secretary in Cleveland, married four years, doesn't need to read Freud to know the truth of his words. "I don't know exactly how to say it. It's something about the difference between having it right there in front of you and something that's not quite in your reach. It's like it gets too easy; all you have to do is reach out and take it. There's no challenge anymore and no more mountains to climb, so some of the excitement is gone. It's too bad, isn't it?" she finished sadly.

No matter how experienced a man or woman may be, sex in the single life represents not just challenge but mystery—the unknown, the uncharted, the illicit. Even among the most liberated, each sexual encounter holds some danger, some test of self, some fear of the vulnerability the sex act evokes. All these are powerful aphrodisiacs; all generate feelings that stimulate and excite. But they all diminish sharply, if they don't actually disappear, once the vows are taken. Trying to explain what happens after marriage, 44-year-old Ralph, a Boston editor, three years into a second marriage, ran a hand through his unruly hair, frowned and said, "The problem is that there's no closed 'paren'; nothing brackets the experience of marriage. The terrible thing about connubial life is that time is endless, and that gives you a whole different sense of time and possibilities. In a relationship that's not 'till death do us part,' you have to make each evening a good one, or else there won't be a next time."

"Or else there won't be a next time"—a phrase that reminds us of the uncertainty men and women experience in their single life. In the period before a commitment is made, people reach for sex for many reasons, not least among them the wish to be reassured that the relationship is theirs. When sex is loaded with the emotional intensity born of insecurity, the experience can be powerful indeed. "Before you're married, it's like an audition," laughed 27-year-old Eve, a Pittsburgh child-care worker, married eight years with two children. "Each time you're together, it's as if you're on trial, like auditioning for the ultimate commitment, I'd guess you'd say. It's a hard time because you always feel so unsure about things, but I think it makes people cling to each other sexually so that bells ring and sparks fly."

Anxiety, which so often accompanies uncertainty, can be a great stimulator of sexual desire as well. Yet it's a link that's rarely explored. Partly that's because we're accustomed to thinking of anxiety as inhibiting rather than inciting sexual appetite. And, in certain circumstances, it most assuredly does just that. But there are other, less obvious reasons why we don't usually connect anxiety with sexual hunger. First, perhaps, is our resistance to the idea, as if it violates some deeply felt taboo to connect sex with anything but romance. Then there's the fact that we like to think of sexual desire as something pure, a unique set of feelings that lives in a realm of its own, feelings different from all others, more powerful, less amenable to our control. Finally, because, as every psychotherapist knows, anxiety shows itself with so many faces, we often don't recognize it for what it is. Therefore, we name it something else.

In discussing masturbation, for example, both men and women frequently remarked that they are most likely to do it when they "need to relax," or "feel edgy," or "get jumpy" or "have trouble sitting still." "It calms me down and gets rid of this feeling I sometimes get where I feel like there's this big lump in my chest," said a 30-year-old house painter in Houston, tapping his chest with his fist as he spoke.

"Do you mean when you feel anxious?"

Looking somewhat baffled, "Yeah, yeah, that's it, isn't it? I guess I never thought of it that way before."

Anxiety plays its part in writing the sexual script when divorce comes into the picture as well. It's not uncommon, for example, for people to report that they had the best sex in years when they knew they were on the verge of a divorce—an experience that often leaves them perplexed and wondering if they're making the right decision. Partly, the renewed sexual excitement may be because this relationship that once seemed without boundary now becomes bracketed. It has an end. But more important, I believe, is that the anxiety about the impending rupture is held in abeyance by an internal psychological process that transforms it into sexual need, lending the encounter a level of excitement and intensity that had been long gone from the marriage bed. "The only time sex was good in my marriage was in the few weeks before we finally separated," recalled a 28-year-old Louisville saleswoman with bewilderment. "I never could figure out why it happened that way. If we could be good at it then, what happened for the four years before that?"

We see it happen, too, when people actually get divorced. Suddenly they become obsessed with sex, experiencing sexual need with a frequency and intensity unknown before. The lived experience is one where sexual craving seems to dominate daily life. But the internal dynamic is something else. There, where the unconscious helps us to ward off feelings we're not ready to handle, anxiety is converted and channeled into sexual desire. The sense of failure, the pain of rejection, the apprehension about our attractiveness and desirability, the fear of the unknown, the need to affirm self in the face of the loss, the loneliness and the emptiness—all these create anxiety that seeks surcease in sex. "When I was divorced, I was always horny. It was like when I was a kid," mused Jerry, a 45-year-old Santa Monica audio technician, who had been remarried for almost three years when we spoke. "It didn't make any difference if there was someone around or not; the feelings were there all the time. It was so intense that I'd sometimes masturbate two and three times a day."

When these difficult and painful issues are resolved, or when the person finds another relationship, sexual appetite retreats, returning to what it had been in periods not so laden with anxiety, uncertainty and fear. "It was amazing," Jerry continued, a bemused smile playing across his lips as he tried to make sense of the experience. "From the time Linda and I moved in together, it all sort of simmered down. We have a great sex life, you understand, but I don't need to be screwing every minute, and I certainly don't think about it all the time. I guess just knowing you have someone there makes a difference; you feel different about yourself, about everything."

The incest taboo also may play a part in the sexual drama of coupled life. One of the hallmarks of our nuclear family is the depth and intensity of the emotional life that exists there. The privacy of the family that we value so highly, the isolation of its members from other sources of sustenance and support, foster bonds of intimacy and dependency between parent and child that are as powerful as any in human life. Only sex is excluded from this intimacy—rigorously, systematically, ruthlessly excluded and denied.[4]

But what is prohibited doesn't cease to exist. It goes underground, into the unconscious, where it waits to return another day. As couples therapists tell their clients, there's always a crowd in the marriage bed—at the very least, the two lovers and the internalized representation of the parents of their childhood, ghosts of mothers and fathers who hover over the action and stir thoughts and feelings long ago pushed out of consciousness.

As adults, we seek relationships in which we can experience once again the powerful feelings of our childhood. Sometimes we are drawn unconsciously to someone who, in one way or another, resembles the parent of those early years. Sometimes we manage to choose someone wholly different. But reality may make little difference here. Psychodynamically, the new family becomes a reenactment of the family of origin, recapitulating both its intensity and its taboos.

For some people, usually those who have had a particularly powerful bond with one or another parent, this can be both wonderful and terrible. The old ecstasy returns and, along with it, the ancient anxiety about the forbidden. "Sometimes when we're right in the middle, I open my eyes and instead of seeing Joe, I see my father's face over me," said 30-year-old Caroline, a Cambridge teacher, her face turning crimson as she spoke. "It's very upsetting when it happens, and I try to shut it out, even though I have to admit that at first I get this tremendous charge. Afterwards, though, it feels terrible, just awful. I've talked to my therapist about it, and he thinks maybe that's why I don't feel very sexual a lot of the time. Joe does look a lot like my dad, you know, the same build even."

For some men, the incest taboo makes itself felt when a nurturing wife becomes a reminder of mother, thereby creating a barrier to the free expression of their sexuality. Ken, a 38-year-old radio newscaster in New Haven, was brought up in a family in which his father was physically absent much of the time and mother was left to dote unhampered on her only son. "It's very hard for me to integrate the concept that you could have very good sex with your wife. I do a lot better with a prostitute or somebody like that," he said, his fingers anxiously plucking imaginary lint from his pants. "With someone who's so important to me, it's very hard to see her as a sexual being."

"Could you try to explain that for me?"

Thinking quietly for a long moment, "Maybe it's that I don't *want* to see her as a sexual being. She's a very supportive and nurturing person, in a sense very mothering, you could say. Maybe it's just plain too scary to have a woman who's like a nurturing mother be sexual at the same time."

Few people are this self-aware, however. Often they know only that they don't feel sexual, that whatever desires they had have somehow disappeared. Sometimes they recognize a vague discomfort, some feeling they can't define that's translated into an inertia about sex they don't understand. "It's like trying to climb over some kind of wall or something. I know the feeling, but I don't understand it, not at all. And believe me, I've tried," said 32-year-old Joan, a San Francisco waitress, married six years. "The crazy thing about it is, when we do it, it feels good; I like it. But there's no carryover."

For some people, the pleasure itself seems like a threat, as if it might unleash feelings that are too wild and explosive to be contained in the context of family life. "I don't know how to say it, but there's something about pleasure," said 32-year-old Meg, a Boston geneticist, reaching for a thought that seemed to elude her. "It's like I'm not supposed to have that much pleasure, especially now that I'm married and a mother," she concluded.

Why is sexual pleasure associated with danger? One reason, certainly, is because the sexual taboos that are so much a part of our childhood family come back to haunt us in the new family of adulthood. As I have already said, when a child's early sexual feelings are expressed in masturbation, they usually are met with disapproval, silence or the remonstrance that this is private, not something permissible in the public space of the family. The response is equally swift and unequivocal when sexual expression is directed outward, away from self, perhaps toward a parent or sibling. This, too, is not acceptable.

For the child, there's bewilderment. What reason can there be for the prohibitions that surround these pleasurable feelings when others are admissible? There rarely are answers to the questions, even if the child dares to ask them. Partly that's because such discussions generally are not a part of family life, and partly, also, because there really are no answers. It's one of those things: it is because it is. This is the nature of a taboo.

Silence sends a message of its own, however—in this case, that there's something about sex and sexual pleasure that threatens the life of the family, that could disrupt relations there. Therefore, it must be confined and contained, hidden from view. For the child, the very idea of sex becomes split off from family life. In adulthood, the new family becomes a reenactment of the earlier one, calling up the old proscriptions that were experienced there. And the split reasserts itself, making it difficult to enjoy sexual pleasure inside the family. "It's like a different kind of incest taboo, not the one we usually talk about," Karen, a 42-year-old New York X-ray technician, explained haltingly. "I'm not sure about this, but maybe what happens is that when you make this new family, you begin to play down your sexual attraction, you know, push it away, just like you did with your brother or parents. Then pretty soon that's how you begin to feel about him, like a brother, not a lover. It's like it's something you shouldn't feel, so you don't. I don't mean you do it consciously, but maybe it just happens."

The need to preserve the integrity of the self, to protect the boundaries that separate self from other, can also create sexual problems in a relationship. For nothing in human life poses the possibility of fusion with another as powerfully as the act of sex. This is what the romantic texts mean when they speak of two people "becoming one," of "melting into each other," of "losing themselves." It's the experience most of us seek—that moment when the boundaries between self and other give way, when the union is complete and we can experience ourselves as one with another. And it's also the one that can be the most frightening, the moment that's most likely to stir ambivalence, if not outright withdrawal.

For some men and women, those who have trouble asserting and protecting their boundaries, the possibility of losing self, even for a moment, can be an unendurable threat. For them, the more intimate the relationship, the greater the peril. "For the last few years I've had a little trouble sexually. Never before that, only since about a year or so after we got married. It's not that we're not close, you understand, because we are, more all the time in lots of ways. But not when it comes to sex, that seems to get harder for us. Well, for me. At first, even when I didn't really want to, my body would go along for the ride. But now it's getting harder to make it cooperate," said 30-year-old Josh, a Denver paramedic, married four years with one child.

Sometimes people develop ways to protect themselves against the merger they fear and continue to enjoy an active sex life with a partner. They may, for example, cultivate a rich fantasy life about others while engaging in sex with a loved mate. The fantasies such people conjure can enhance sexual pleasure while also keeping them sufficiently distanced from the interaction at hand so that they feel safe from the threat of boundary loss.

But for whatever reasons—perhaps a lack of psychological resiliency, perhaps a lack of imagination—such adaptations aren't available to everyone for whom the fear of fusion with another inhibits sexual activity or performance. Some who suffer this fear will report they do better in sex with someone who means little or nothing to them than with one they love. "It's funny, of the men I've had real relationships with, including my husband, the best sex I ever had was with the guy I was least attached to," said 41-year-old Nancy, a paralegal in Syracuse, married ten years with two children.

Such people will tend to avoid sex as attachment and intimacy grow. When the fear reaches obviously pathological proportions—a man who can't ejaculate, or one who has lost all sexual desire; a woman who's phobic about vaginal penetration, or one who becomes wholly inorgasmic—people may seek psychotherapeutic help. But most of the time it gets written off to time and pressure, to a problem where the head and the body just can't seem to get together.

Interestingly, most of the couples who complained about the decline of sexual interest and activity in their daily lives also often told of sharp increases when they're on vacation. A patterned shift that, on the surface, seems to validate the notion that time and pressure are key culprits in the waning of sex after marriage. "There's a real difference when we go on vacation, which, unfortunately, isn't very often. But when we do, we have sex almost every day," said 29-year-old Robin, a swimming coach in Santa Barbara, married six years with one child. "It's wonderful, even though we're still not as playful or experimental as we used to be."

Without doubt the relaxation a vacation permits is a central factor in the intensification of sexual interest. It's not external situational pressures alone that abate, however, but internal psychological ones as well. In the daily life of which I have been speaking, there's an erosion of a sense of self as well as time, a feeling that the unique and identifiable self we once knew has gotten lost, absorbed into the demands and distractions of the several roles we play each day. The end of the day is a time for reclamation, for pulling the day's fragmented self together into a coherent whole once again. Losing oneself in the intimacy of sex, then, can feel more like a threat than a promise, too anxiety-provoking to pursue with ease and pleasure. "I can't really explain it, but I sometimes feel like I have to make a choice between sex and me, if you know what I mean," remarked Dorothy, a 32-year-old Charleston beautician.

By easing such pressures, vacations allow people to experience themselves in a more fully integrated way throughout the day. Rather than meeting the very idea of sex with resistance, they are freed to bring themselves to it with anticipation, savoring the experience once again, feeling the excitement and pleasure they so often miss in their lives at home.

For some people, the unfamiliarity of the vacation life and setting can itself be liberating, allowing them to step out of their usual roles and relationships and to release an aspect of self not ordinarily seen or heard from. It's well known, however, that, for many people, this very unfamiliarity increases anxiety, since they are denied the normal activities, people and objects through which they define themselves in their everyday life. Either way, sex life gets a boost. For those whose constraints are released by the unfamiliar, there's license for the kind of sexual expression, even the evocation of fantasy, that life at home forecloses. For those whose anxiety is heightened, sex with a known and loved partner can serve to connect them once again to the self that seems to have been displaced.

One way out of confronting some of the binds people experience in their coupled sex life is a very old one—sexual activity outside the relationship. Among the women and men who had been divorced, almost all had done just that during the marriage, often more than once.[5] For most of them, it was the beginning of the end of the marriage. "The affair I had was very brief and upset me for a number of reasons—because it ended, because it began and mostly because it showed me very distinctly that I had a much stronger desire for someone outside my relationship than in it," said 39-year-old Stephen, a Chicago bartender.

Others said they already knew the relationship was at an end when they succumbed to temptation. But they weren't quite ready to make the final break. "In both cases, the men were very sweet, gentle, nonthreatening, sensitive guys, which was the opposite of the man I was married to," said 36-year-old Eileen, a Columbus bookkeeper. "I knew before I ever got involved with either one of them that I'd have to get out of the marriage, but it took a while to get myself to leave, and the affairs made it tolerable to stay."

Over 40 percent of the men and women who were still married admitted to at least one extramarital sexual liaison—sometimes an affair, sometimes a casual encounter, sometimes with a prostitute. The figure for those who were living together in committed relationships was substantially less, just over a quarter, perhaps because for them there are fewer social and institutional pressures to keep them from simply changing partners.

Sometimes a mate acted in retaliation against the other. "Jon had one brief affair that I know of; it was with someone we both knew," said Judy, a 31-year-old Louisville computer sales-woman, in a rush of words. Then pausing as if for emphasis, she gave a short, ironic laugh and continued: "She was a good friend of mine. I tried to be understanding, but it hurt too much. I felt so betrayed by both of them. At about that time I ran into this very attractive guy I sort of knew, but hadn't seen for a long time. He came on strong to me, and I thought: 'Fuck it, why not? I don't owe Jon anything after what he did.' So we had this real heavy thing for a couple of months."

A few people said that these relationships outside the marriage allowed them to stay in it without feelings of discontent or deprivation. "It picks up some of the pieces that get dropped with Jo," said 32-year-old Nick, a San Jose salesman, who has been married for six years.

"Can you explain what you mean by that?"

"Sure, I love Jo, but she's not as available sexually as I need her to be, and I'm not about to be begging. Some guys are always fighting over that with their wives or girlfriends. I just go and get a little somewhere else. I like it; it reminds me I'm a desirable guy. You can forget that sometimes when you've been together as long as Jo and I have."

"Does JoAnn know about this?"

"Christ, no, and I don't want her to either, for two reasons. First of all, I don't want to hurt her. And," he continued with a mischievous grin after a pause, "because I don't want her to get any ideas about doing the same thing."

But JoAnn, a lab technician, had a different story to tell.[6] Leaning back in her chair, she lit a cigarette and said very deliberately, "I don't know if Nick told you that he has affairs once in a while. He thinks I don't know, but as you can see, I do."

"Why are you telling me this?" I wondered.

"Because you asked me if I'd ever had sex outside my marriage, and I thought Nick might not have told you, and I wanted you to know the whole story before I answer your question."

"That's a good reason. Now can you answer my question?"

"Yes, and yes. I've been with two other men since Nick and I have been married, brief affairs, but not inconsequential. You see, I love Nick; he's really a good man, and I plan to live with him for the rest of my life. But he's just not a wonderful lover. I sometimes think the sexual revolution cost us a lot. If I hadn't had all those other experiences, I wouldn't have anything to compare it to and wouldn't know what I was missing. But they *are* part of my life, and I can't pretend I don't know. So when the opportunity presents itself for something that will be a really fully satisfying experience, I take it. It doesn't happen often, as you can see, probably because most men just aren't that good sexually. When you've had as much experience as I have, you can usually tell even before you actually try them out. You know a lot by the way they handle the preliminaries."

"With all your experience, why can't you teach Nick?"

With an impatient sigh, "I'm not sure you ought to be the one writing this book if you have to ask that question."

"But I am," I laughed, "so could you help me by answering it?"

"I've tried to teach him, but I've come to the firm belief that there are things you can't teach, and being sensual and appreciating sensuality is one of them. Nick's prick works fine, but the rest, well . . . Don't get me wrong, he tries. He'll do anything I tell him, but that's not the point, because if it's not something that's coming from inside him, then it doesn't mean much to me. But we don't fight about it like other people do. I pretty much control the pace of our sex life, and he does what he has to do about it. As long as it doesn't interfere with the rest of our lives, I don't care."

"Then why is it a secret?"

"I think Nick needs to believe that I'd be devastated, so we leave it that way."

In fact, there's a tolerance for extramarital sex that's surprising.

I don't mean to suggest that people encourage it or that there are no feelings of betrayal when a transgression becomes known. But perhaps because these veterans of the sexual revolution have themselves had such broad-ranging experiences, they attribute less importance to them. Perhaps also, because their own taste for sexual variety is so well developed, they assume that the time will come, for them or for their mate, when the thrill of the chase and the excitement of being pursued will be too tempting to resist. As one recently married 24-year-old woman in Trenton, New Jersey, said: "It's hard to imagine that Jimmy will be the last guy I'll ever sleep with. I just assume that if I'm married to him for the rest of my life, there'll be some opportunities I won't want to miss."

Three of the sixty married couples (5 percent) had experimented with open marriages, all of them old hands of the early days of the sexual revolution. Not surprisingly, it was a different experience for the wives and for the husbands. All agreed that, even when the woman was wholly open to the idea, it presented more conflicts for her than for him. And in each case, he was much more active outside the marriage than she was. "We both thought it was a good idea, but I don't know if I'd ever have done it if Marty hadn't pushed it," Kathy, a 42-year-old insurance actuary from Milwaukee, explained. "It was titillating to think about, but doing it, that was something else. Once we decided, though, I got into it. But we went at it differently. He really fucked around, and I was much more selective about who I went to bed with. There was always someone around he had a hard on for, but I couldn't be just fucking some guy because he had a great body."

For one couple, the decision to open the marriage came after serious conflict about the husband's affair with another woman. "We separated for a few months because I was seeing another woman and she couldn't stand it," recalled 38-year-old Phil, a Washington lobbyist. "When we got back together again, I came clean about everything I'd been up to before, and we decided the marriage should be more open. The effect of that was to take away a lot of the pressure and frustration I'd been feeling about being tied down, so nothing much happened for a long while after that.

"If we'd stayed in Wisconsin, I think that's the way it would have been. But then we moved here to D.C., and it's a lot more sexually charged atmosphere here than I'd known before, and my wife and I got involved in all kinds of things. At one point we wound up having a sexual relationship with another couple. It was like all my fantasies come true. But then the roof fell in because I met my second wife and fell in love. I really don't know if that marriage would have ended by itself. I've never had a better sexual relationship than with my first wife. Nothing was ever difficult with her, and we were extremely compatible. And thinking about the fantasy thing you asked about before, when I was with other women, including my second wife, I used to fantasize all the time about being with my first wife. Thank God, I don't do that anymore."

Only one of the three open marriages survives, but not without renegotiating the rules of the marriage so that it is now wholly monogamous. "It turned out to be fuck now, pay later," said 40-year-old Caroline, the owner of a gift shop in suburban Los Angeles, married sixteen years with two children. "What we always said would never happen, happened. I fell in love with one of those outsiders. It wasn't supposed to be part of the game, but it happened, and we separated for about a year while I lived with this other man. It was during that time that I understood that if Andy and I were going to get back together again, we'd have to go to a totally monogamous relationship, and that was nonnegotiable."

I asked her husband, a 41-year-old economic analyst, "Do you wish sometimes you could have an open marriage again?"

"No. It's too hard to pull off. I find myself thinking: Do I regret that we did it? It led to a separation, and in that sense I do. But when I think about it, I feel like I gained a lot from it, even though it ended up being terribly painful. Part of it may have to do with age. Once you've been through a series of experiences, no matter how fondly you may remember them, you don't necessarily have to repeat them."

What happens to sexual passion when couples live together without marriage? In their 1983 study, Philip Blumstein and Pepper Schwartz found that 61 percent of unmarried couples living together for less than two years had sex three times a week or more, while among married couples of the same vintage, the figure was 45 percent.[7] As the years together increase, the incidence of sexual activity decreases sharply for both, and the gap between the two groups narrows substantially.[8] Among the cohabiting couples I interviewed, there generally were fewer complaints about the quality of their sexual interaction than among those who were married. But most were relationships of relatively short duration—a median of two years, compared with five years for the marrieds—and only two had children. Still, it seems worth exploring the differences.

Part of the difference, perhaps, is that even when couples talk about a lifetime commitment, there's something different in the internal experience of living together as opposed to being married. "It just feels different to know you're together because this is what you really want, and not because you've made that ridiculous public display and gotten hooked into all the legal and institutional stuff that surrounds marriage," said 33-year-old Paul, a furniture refinisher in Raleigh, who has been living with his partner, Diana, for four years. "It also keeps you from getting too smug," he concluded. By which he meant there's a certain tentativeness to the relationship that doesn't allow the partners to take it for granted.

But what's different in marriage these days? Surely staying married is not something anyone takes for granted anymore. But truth or reality makes little difference here. For, as an old sociological adage insists: "If the situation is defined as real, then it is real in its consequences." And the *internal* definition of the situation is different when people are living together than when they are married, with the former usually being experienced as less permanent, more vulnerable to whim and fancy than the latter.[9] If it weren't so, why would people who have lived together for years suddenly feel the need to marry? "We were living together for four years when we decided to get married," said 33-year-old Sally, a Detroit purchasing agent, married two years. "We both thought it was time to make that kind of public statement. Getting married meant making that final commitment."

Speaking rapidly and in a voice charged with emotional intensity, her husband, Charles, the owner of a bar, agreed and added, "Getting married seemed to make everything more," hesitating as he searched for a word, "important—I guess that's the word—important. It separated it from just being an affair. It said, okay this is valid; this is real; this is the way it's supposed to be. You go through this ceremony in front of people and sign papers and watch them put all the official stamps on them. It does something; it changes you."

The words themselves—"living together" and "married"— have a different ring, suggest a different cast to the relationship. One focuses on the act of living and relating, the other on the institution; one suggests a process, the other a fait accompli. An important part of a biography is written in the words "We're married"—a personal biography as well as a social statement. If we know nothing more about people than that they're married, we already know that they've made a serious commitment to each other, one they can't abandon without some social consequences.

But the phrase "living together" is ambiguous, defining neither a state of mind nor a state of being, telling us nothing about the commitments or lack of them a relationship embodies. For some people, living together is transient, more important than going together but not a serious commitment. For some, it's a trial run, a test before embarking on the real thing. For still others, it's a commitment as deep as a formal marriage but, for whatever reasons in their own history, it *feels* different to them. "The major reason we're not married is that it's more fun not to be. There's a slight edge in the relationship this way, and it's good to keep it like that. It tends to keep things more alive," said 40-year-old Marge, a San Francisco writer, who has one child with her partner, Richard, which whom she's lived for three years.

With all the difficulties that exist in long-term committed relationships, however, there's little doubt that, whether married or living together, for most people, sex is freer and more varied than ever before. Many of the couples I met, more often those under 35 than those who were older, talked easily and freely about masturbating together—"We love to watch each other masturbate; it's a great turn-on"; about sharing their private sexual fantasies—"It's very exciting to tell our fantasies to each other while we're making love"; about varying the time, place and manner of their sexual encounters—"We keep trying different things and new places to keep things lively, you know, to keep sex from getting boring"; about watching pornographic films together—"I bring home a film about once a week or so, and we'll spend most of the night in bed, eating and watching and making love." All these ways and more serve to invigorate and enhance sexual interactions.

While communication about sexual needs and wishes is still difficult for most people, they generally are aware of the need to be more open with each other and many say they work at it. "It's very hard to break sexual patterns, since you developed them because that's what you're comfortable with, even if they don't always satisfy you," said 32-year-old Judi Anne, a legal secretary in New Haven, married seven years. "But we knew we had to, so in the last couple of years we've been trying to explore different ways to be more intimate sexually. It's very slow, very hard, when you're trying to get to a new place, and we're not there yet. To change communication about anything is very hard for us, and when you're dealing with something as raw as sex, it's even harder. But we're plugging along, and that's really what counts—that we keep trying."

Yet as time takes its toll on sexual frequency, intensity and passion, many couples who otherwise have no complaints continue to ask anxiously, "What happened?" As I struggled to make sense of their lives and their questions, it seemed to me worth turning the question around. Instead of wondering what happens in marriage to mute sexual passion, perhaps the question we need to answer is: Why is the level of sexual tension and activity so high before marriage?

Looked at that way, we might conclude that, given the intense emphasis on sex and sexuality over these last decades, sex has come to be experienced as *the* arena for the expression and satisfaction of a whole rainbow of needs and yearnings that go well beyond sexual pleasure—from comfort and support to affirmation of self; from attachment and connection to security and continuity. A committed relationship reassures us, offering as it does the promise that those needs will be met. Therefore, their clamorous demands abate, and sexual desire is no longer experienced with such urgency and intensity.

I don't mean to disparage the reality that there's some genuine loss when sexual excitement declines, just as there is when we lose the wildly obsessive feelings we knew when we first fell in love. Yet no one expects those feelings to continue unabated. Why is it different with sex? Why is it that so many men and women who talk eloquently about the gains in their marriage still can't wholly put away their doubt and regret about sex. "I don't exactly know how to say it. Maybe we don't do it as often now because we're right there all the time and you don't have to grab the moment. I miss that, but I also know that getting married validated sex in ways I never expected, so in some ways it's better," said 37-year-old Curt, a Cleveland building contractor, married three years. "I feel more secure, safe; I trust her more. I feel I can do anything and still be accepted. I can bring home porn movies or a donkey, and she might not want to join me in it, but she wouldn't abandon me. When I talk about it, it reminds me how unsafe and unsatisfying those casual affairs and one-night stands were, even though sometimes they were very exciting. So what the hell do I miss?"

His wife, who told of a wide variety of sexual experiences before her marriage, said, "Safe, that's the first word that comes when I think about how sex changed after we got together. That's one thing I never felt with all that screwing around I did. He's the first man I've ever trusted, I mean, *really* trusted, so sex

feels, how can I say it, deeper, more intimate, I guess. Everything feels more solid, so sex does, too."

"Then you're not troubled by the decline in frequency of sex
or a lessening of intensity?"

With a sad smile, "I wish I could say that's true. I tell myself
more isn't better, but I think we both worry about it a little . . .
well, maybe more than a little. How could you not worry about
it? Everything around you makes such a big thing of that kind
of passion—the movies, TV, wherever you go you see these
steamy scenes, and you can't help wondering if maybe something's wrong because you're not feeling that way all the time,
or maybe we should be doing more to try to jack it up and make
it more like it was."

Repeatedly I heard the same refrain—women and men who
are torn, fearful that something may be amiss, that they're not
attending to some signal that warns of trouble. How can it be
otherwise when we're exhorted at every turn to strive for some
unnamed sexual perfection, some kind of never-ending ecstasy?
Hundreds of books, many of them national best-sellers, are dedicated to aiding us in our search for more and greater sexual
pleasure, telling us in words and pictures how to achieve it. At
last count, the Doubleday bookstore on Fifth Avenue in New
York City had almost two hundred volumes in its section on sex
alone, not to mention the hundreds more elsewhere in the store
that deal with sex as one of the many issues that beset our
relationships. Each month the glossy magazines have yet another
article about sex, while newspapers headline surveys announcing
one day that "Women Want More Sex" and a short time later
that "Men Want More Sex."[10] All creating external pressures
about sex and how it ought to be, which, in turn, raise internal
doubts that bedevil our days and interfere with our nights.

Sex therapists and other experts tell us we don't know enough,
don't talk enough. We must learn more, communicate more,
still the inhibitions that keep us from telling each other what we
want and need, they counsel. Important and useful advice, no
doubt. But if talk itself is so useful, why is it that, despite all
the talk, despite all the information put before us, our sexual

difficulties continue to support a thriving sex therapy business? Could it be that all the noise about sex has served mainly to foster uneasiness and confusion, while also helping to create a set of impossible expectations? Could it be that we're in danger of talking too much, of discussing and explaining away the mystery, the adventure, the sense of exploration and discovery that's so much a part of the excitement of sex? Indeed, I wonder if the incessant talk isn't at least part of the problem that underlies the lack of desire that is now increasingly being brought to the consulting rooms of sex therapists all across the country.

Ironically, with all the public talk about sex, the private realm remains shrouded in silence and mystery. I saw it repeatedly in the interviews—people comparing themselves with others, with things they've seen, heard and read; asking me whether this or that behavior was normal; wanting to know how often "most people" have sex after two years, five years, ten years of marriage; fearing that they may be failing where others are succeeding. Anxieties that leave us preoccupied with the state of the relationship, fearful we might lose the very security we thought we had. Anxieties at least in part born of the mystery about sex, which, as philosopher Edmund Leites has written, "is in large part a function of affirming it to be unceasingly active . . . even when it appears to be absent."[11]

It makes no difference whether or not we personally experience our sex lives as deficient. We find ourselves grappling with a set of impossible expectations, with some standard "out there" against which we measure ourselves. For we live now with a new sexual dogma that allows for as little deviation as the old one did, one that calls us to a relentless preoccupation with the content and quality of our sexual interactions. Paradoxically, our absorption with what's wrong and how to fix it creates its own problems. And sex becomes another issue that needs time and attention, another obstacle to be overcome, instead of a time out for gratification and pleasure.

1. Jessie Bernard, *The Future of Marriage* (New York: Bantam Books, 1973).
2. April 24, 1989, pp. 58–67.
3. Sigmund Freud, *Three Essays on the Theory of Sexuality* (New York: Avon Books, 1962). Edmund Leites, in *The Puritan Conscience and Modern Sexuality* (New Haven: Yale University Press, 1986), writes that in the second half of the seventeenth century a major theme in English comedy was the elaboration of the belief that in marriage "the price of constancy, fidelity, and steadiness of feeling is the sacrifice of intense excitement, at least in the sexual arena and perhaps in others as well" (p. 14).
4. I am, of course, aware of the large numbers of cases of sexual abuse in families. But these only mean that the incest taboo has been broken, not that it doesn't exist and play a powerful role in our conscious and unconscious sexual choices. Indeed, the shame and guilt that accompany an incestuous relationship are themselves evidence of the power of the taboo, as is the fact that we label it "abuse" and call it a crime.
5. See Annette Lawson, *Adultery* (New York: Basic Books, 1988) for an interesting study of adultery.
6. Obviously, all identifying information has been changed here, as in all the other quotes throughout this book. Nevertheless, in this case, since I used such an extended quotation from the lives of this couple, it seemed to me that one or both might recognize themselves. Therefore, I showed each of them the pages that contain their side of the dialogue before publication. After suggesting some changes that each felt might ensure his/her anonymity—changes that didn't substantively alter the sense or content of the story—both gave their permission for its publication as it appears here. Still concerned that there might be some fallout to their marriage when the book is published, I pressed them to think carefully about the possible consequences. Both said the interview had stimulated them to deal more directly with the issues between them and that they had been trying to do so. And each in his/her own way suggested that it might be "a relief to get it all out in the open."
7. *American Couples* (New York: William Morrow, 1983).
8. Blumstein and Schwartz, *American Couples*. Among those living together from two to ten years, 38 percent of the cohabitants had sex three times a week, compared with 27 percent of the marrieds.
9. The Blumstein and Schwartz sample had no couples who were living together more than ten years. My own had only one cohabiting couple who were together for as long as six years—figures which, in themselves, suggest a greater level of instability in cohabiting couples than in those who are married.
10. See the San Francisco *Chronicle*, which on March 15, 1988, headlined the results of a *Glamour* magazine survey: "Poll Finds Women Want More Sex." Fifty-six percent of the women who were married or had regular

partners "said they would like to have sex more often," the poll results showed. One year later, on March 15, 1989, the same newspaper headlined another poll by the same magazine: "Survey: Men Want More Sex." Then we learned that "46 percent of the women said they were very satisfied with their sex lives," while 51 percent of the men said they would like to have sex more often.

11. *The Puritan Conscience and Modern Sexuality*, p. 144.

# 9

———◆———

# Waves, Ripples and Rocks on the Shore

*A* book calls for a conclusion, words that sum it up, that tie
the loose ends into a neat package. But a social movement is
like life—unruly, unpredictable, defying easy categories or neat
endings. At the beginning, the sexual revolution washed over
us like a great wave, crashing over the rocks on the shore,
sweeping aside the debris that had lain there for decades, erasing
the footprints of the past that had been etched so deeply in the
sand. When the wave receded, the sand lay sparkling in the
sun, smoothed clean, ready for a new beginning. But the rocks
were still there, their contours somewhat eroded by the force
of the water, a new shape emerging but not yet quite formed.

It seemed for a while as if the sexual revolution might accomplish what others had not, a revolution in which everybody won.
If sexual pleasure is a good, then a win-win outcome looked
possible. There was more of it around, and it was more equitably
distributed. For women, it meant freedom from the sexual constraints under which they had lived for so long. For men, it

meant sexual access to a wider range of women than had ever before been available.

For a while, both feasted on their newfound freedoms. Women eagerly embraced the sexual experimentation and exploration that became possible, taking to themselves many of the prerogatives that had, until then, been for men only. Men roamed this vastly enlarged sexual marketplace, sampling its wares hungrily, reveling in a variety that had existed only in their wildest fantasies before.

But for women, the revolution soon foundered on the rocks on the shore. There were new footprints in the sand, to be sure. But the old ones, it turned out, had not been erased at all; they were only covered over for a time. The boundaries of acceptable sexual expression for women had been significantly broadened, but the structure of social relations within which their sexual interactions were taking place remained relatively untouched.

For some of the women I met, therefore, especially those who want to marry but who face men who seem so resistant, the very words "sexual revolution" came to sound like a mockery. "Men can do all that screwing around and it doesn't matter, but I think women are damaged by it," said 38-year-old Gloria, a New York magazine executive, her voice etched with pain and bitterness. "There were a lot of power games going on that hurt women a lot. I don't want to sound like one of those awful Moral Majority people, but I think I let some of my power go by having sex as freely as I've done. Women had a lot more leverage with men before sex got so free."

"Are you saying that if you'd been less available sexually, you might have had a better chance at the kind of committed relationship you now want?"

"I don't think that individually; I think that collectively. I mean, I don't look back and think that there's this particular relationship that didn't work out but that might have worked if I'd been less sexually available. But I think if women in general were less available sexually, I might be in a relationship, and so would a lot of other women who are feeling deprived now."

Sex as leverage—an old story in the balance of power between men and women, a script that called for a woman to withhold sex until a man capitulated. Conservative critics of the feminist movement long ago warned that, by giving up this most powerful weapon, women would be seriously disadvantaging themselves in the marriage market. Were they less naïve about the potential for equality in personal relations between women and men than their feminist sisters?

Most of the men I spoke with denied that they would feel greater pressure to make commitments, whether in marriage or not, if sex weren't so freely available. "Christ, that's nuts. What would sex have to do with that?" demanded a 32-year-old tile setter. Some thought about it, but decided they couldn't know. "How would I know that?" asked a 29-year-old automobile mechanic, puzzlement wrinkling his brow. "I've never lived in a time when you couldn't have sex when you wanted it." About one-third agreed. "If women were less sexually available, I'd be married by now," said a 25-year-old computer technician without hesitation. "I'm not complaining about that; I'm just saying that because they're so sexually available, I find myself tempted to stay single, to try it all out, so to speak."

Even some of older men who had already "tried it all out" gave reluctant assent. "Well, maybe it's not sex *qua* sex," mused 47-year-old Adam, a Berkeley doctor, "but it's so easy to have a woman's companionship now that there's not a great push to pin it down like there used to be. I've been divorced for five years, and I don't know what I'm going to do about marriage. There's a feast out there and, well, maybe you get sated with all that food, so you stop eating for a little while. But I don't feel a great need to get hooked up with someone like I did when I got married before."

It's ironic, isn't it? Feminists, who have been accused of hating men, believed enough in their goodwill to engage with them in a struggle for change. It's the New Right conservatives, those women who have been lauded as the epitome of compliant femininity, who are the cynical and distrustful ones, the real hardliners. It's these women who cry out about male perfidy, who insist that only under duress can men be expected to behave responsibly. It's they who talk about the need to confine men more tightly in their roles lest their restless and rebellious nature leads them astray; the same women who applaud when one of their leaders proclaims that "men desire sex without responsibility" and that if their wish is granted, they will inevitably escape the net women must prepare for them. "They become unmanly and frightened by the thought of having to assume economic responsibility for a family: They instinctively try to escape."[1] A more cynical view of men than the most ardent feminist is likely to hold.

But the argument that men resist marriage because of the easy availability of sex today is far too simple. At the most obvious level, it places the sexual revolution at the center of relations between women and men while ignoring the impact of the gender revolution. Yet it is the latter that has had the most profound influence on both public and private life.

Just as women are no longer demure, asexual maidens awaiting their awakening by the man of their dreams, so they are not just wives, mothers, clerks and secretaries. Suddenly, they no longer accept their traditional roles as given in nature, no longer believe they are the inferior ones, incapable of full adulthood. Suddenly, they are active competitors in the world of work, coveting jobs that, until recently, belonged to men alone. Suddenly, they are asking men to participate in the life of the family in whole new ways, from rearing the children to doing the laundry to joining them in the struggle for more open and intimate communication. It's all these that have revolutionized our relations with each other, that are at the center of our conflicts around family life today.

When I hear the criticism of the sexual revolution now being voiced by both feminists and their enemies, I'm inclined to ask: Compared with what? Certainly the problems we face today are different from those of yesterday. But are they worse? Was there really a time when women had a better, more secure life than the one we know now? If so, when was it? A century ago, when, because good women were defined as asexual, their respectable, middle-class husbands regularly visited prostitutes and equally regularly infected their wives with the venereal diseases they contracted there? Or when life in the family was guided by the voice of the father, the patriarch, and women and children were little more than his property, to be used and disposed of at his will?

Was it better in our more recent past, in the fifties, when men complained endlessly about the sexual inhibitions of their wives? Or when the big issue concerning the sex experts was what they called women's "frigidity"? Or when stories about the "trapped housewife" became big news, filling both TV screens and the pages of magazines and newspapers across the land? Or when the word "depression" called up images of the married women who kept the practices of psychologists and psychiatrists flourishing?

If this, indeed, was a better time, why did the ideas promulgated by the feminists of the late sixties and early seventies spread to such unlikely places with such lightning speed? Why did they find resonance in the hearts and minds of women who, to this day, would refuse to accept the feminist label as their own? It wasn't feminists who drove women into the work force in ever-increasing numbers; who were responsible for the escalating divorce rates; who created the discontent so many women experienced with the confines of the "feminine mystique";[2] who lengthened the life span at the same time that family size decreased, leaving women with half their lives before them after the children left home. All these were in place before the first stirrings were heard from the feminist front. Each played its part in the creation of the women's movement and in driving it forward.

As we find ourselves confronting an escalating spiral of change, we long for what, from a distance, seems like the comfort and certainty of the past. But the notion that there was a golden age of the family, a time when women and men contentedly played out their roles as given, when female chastity resolved the sexual conflicts between women and men, expresses not a reality about the past, but a longing for a world that exists in imagination alone. For neither the sexual nor the gender revolution could have taken root if life, whether inside the family or out, had been as utopian as nostalgia would have it. Such a widespread attack on the norms and values of an age can take place only when disaffection with the existing order is wide and deep, when the problems of living are no longer amenable to the solutions available.

Yes, life probably was less complicated in those earlier times, but simpler doesn't mean better. And the pain we know today is not made any easier by the glorification of a yesterday that by now has gained mythic proportions. Looking backward with longing may assuage the distress of our helplessness for a moment. It allows us to believe that there were answers then, that if we can return to that time, hope will be restored. But the images we conjure are not only unreal, they are useless in the present reality, no help at all in getting us into the kinds of relationships that will bring us the satisfaction we want and need.

No revolution creates a wholly new universe. Rather, it reflects the history and culture that spawned it. So it is with the sexual revolution. From our earliest beginnings, we have been a nation obsessed with sex, titillated by it at the same time that we fear it, elaborating rules to contain it at the same time that we violate them. Is it any wonder that a generation of angry, alienated young chose this arena in which to show their profound contempt for the values and hypocrisies of the society that gave them life?

Despite the extraordinary changes their efforts wrought, however, the sexual revolution could not wholly escape its heritage. It wasn't long, therefore, before the revolution began to exhibit the same compulsive obsession with sex that characterized the society that produced it, only this time the avowed purpose was to embrace sex, not to contain it. Not surprisingly, the celebration of sex for its own sake has turned out to have its own problems. And we have found ourselves left with a peculiar malaise, a haunting hunger that, no matter how often and how much, sex alone cannot satisfy. We feel empty in the midst of plenty; we long for something to fill the void, but it continues to elude us.

What Bertrand Russell had to say about the quality of American life in the 1920s aptly describes our recent past as well. "Pleasure is frantic and bacchanalian," he wrote, "a matter of momentary oblivion, not of delightful self-expression."[3] Sex, alcohol, drugs—all these have brought us "momentary oblivion" in our own time. Like the compulsive binge eater, we have continued to consume sex in great gobs, each time experiencing the moment of oblivion, the exquisite release from the need that drives us, only to find the need unfulfilled, the hunger unsatisfied. And we eat again.

Finally, we understand that eating alone will not appease the hunger we feel. The task, we now know, is to find our way from the fleeting encounters that have left us so unsatisfied to the kinds of relationships we want and need. To accomplish this, we must understand also that our relationship to our sexuality is intimately connected to our roles as men and women; both are deeply rooted in our internal life. It was naïve to think that such thoroughly internalized values and beliefs, such historic ways of seeing the world and being in it, would give way easily. Indeed, coming to terms with the reality that psychological change will not follow automatically on the heels of social change is one of the most difficult problems all revolutionary movements must confront. For while our internal psychological life is born in and nurtured by the structure of social relations, that psychology ultimately emerges with a life of its own, an independent and compelling force that must be dealt with in its own terms.

It's no surprise, therefore, that the gains in the public sector, inadequate though they may yet be, have far exceeded those in the private realm. For the deeper, more difficult problem lies in changing what happens inside ourselves, in the regions of the mind and heart that are not accessible to reason, logic or law, the place where feeling reigns supreme.

Am I suggesting, then, that social change must await psychological change? Emphatically not. My argument is simply that the two go hand in hand, and that attempts to change the social structures within which our private lives are embedded will have only limited success unless we give equally serious attention to the psychological barriers that stand in the way. And in no facet of our lives are the sociological and psychological more deeply entwined. For, as Jeffrey Weeks has written: "Sex is the most private thing about us, and the factor that has the most profound social significance."[4]

But it is never sex alone that is under discussion or attack; it is the whole panoply of gender relationships that are at stake. Stated in its simplest form, the mandate for female chastity gave men virtual ownership of women. In return, women were promised a lifetime of male support and protection. This is the underlying bargain in marriage and family life in the modern age, the social contract that helped put women in the home and left men free for activities outside it.

Never mind that it hasn't always worked that way; never mind that, in this era, the bargain is violated at least as often as it's honored. The promise remains a seductive one for substantial numbers of women as well as men. It shouldn't surprise us, then, that nothing engages our feelings more quickly or more deeply than attempts to reorder the sexual contract, or that no issue in American life is more likely to become embroiled in the politics of an age.

When, therefore, the governor of California decimates the already slim budget of the state's Office of Family Planning, it is not simply budgetary considerations or program effectiveness that motivates his action. It is an attempt to strike a blow for female sexual chastity and all it stands for. Just so, it's not simply pro-life or pro-choice, as the fight around abortion has come to be labeled. Whatever the other concerns on both sides, the intensity of the debate, the heat it has generated, turns on the issue of female sexuality—on whether a woman has the right to be sexually free without untoward consequence, and on what the cost will be to the traditional structure of gender relationships.

The moralists among us rejoice as they herald what they see as a new sexual conservatism abroad today. But, in fact, the changes wrought by the sexual revolution have penetrated so deeply into our society that the traditional words to describe sexual trends—"liberalism," "conservatism," "chastity"—no longer fit. What does it mean to talk about a return to sexual conservatism when over two-thirds of the nation's teenagers are sexually active? How do we distinguish the sexual liberals from the conservatives when churches of the Christian Right hold Marriage Encounter weekends in which couples are taught ways to enhance communication in order to keep the sexual fires alive in marriage?

The great wave of the 1960s and 1970s has receded. But its ripples continue to make themselves felt not just in our sexual behavior but in the whole mind-set we bring to sexuality today, in the continuing expansion of the borders of the acceptable, even among the generations who were not themselves part of the sexual revolution. A few weeks ago, for example, I talked with a convent-educated woman in her mid-fifties who commented with the utmost casualness that her 22-year-old daughter was living with her boyfriend. When I remarked on the ease with which she seemed to accept a situation so at odds with the training of her own past, she laughed and said, "If you think that's surprising, what would you think of my 79-year-old Catholic mother who invites them to dinner?"

At the other end of the age spectrum, on the day after the U.S. Supreme Court returned to the states the power to circumscribe access to abortion, I spoke with a 16-year-old who said angrily, "They can't do that! All my life abortion has been legal, now they can't make it illegal all of a sudden like that." *They* can, of course. But not without alienating and enraging a younger generation who take such rights for granted, neither more nor less than part of the universe they inhabit.

There are countercurrents, to be sure—powerful ones set in motion by a highly vocal, well-organized minority who come to the fight against sexual freedom and the changing gender roles with all the fervor of committed religionists. Nevertheless, what we are witnessing in this period is not a return to an outdated past, but a thoughtful pause, a moment of consolidation, an attempt, difficult though it may be, to reorder our relationships, sexual and otherwise, in ways that will bring more lasting satisfaction to us all. The sexual revolution has not been turned back, but the quest for meaning has joined sex at center stage.

And the ripples continue, slowly but inexorably eroding the rocks on the shore.

———————————◆————————————

1. Randy Engel, "The Family Under Siege," *American Life Lobby*, Fall 1980:
   1. Quoted in Barbara Ehrenreich, Elizabeth Hess and Gloria Jacobs, *Remaking Love: The Feminization of Sex* (Garden City, N.Y.: Anchor Books, 1987), p. 147.
2. See Betty Friedan's now classic *The Feminine Mystique* (New York: W. W. Norton, 1963).
3. Bertrand Russell, *Marriage and Morals* (New York: Bantam Books, 1959).
4. Jeffrey Weeks, *Sexuality and Its Discontents* (London: Routledge & Kegan Paul, 1985), p. 80.

# Bibliography

Alexander, Cheryl S. et al. "Early Sexual Activity Among Adolescents in Small Towns and Rural Areas." *Family Planning Perspectives* 21, 6 (November/December, 1989): 261–266.

Allen, Frederick Lewis. *Only Yesterday.* New York: Harper & Brothers, 1957.

Ariès, Philippe, and André Béjin. *Western Sexuality: Practice and Precept in Past and Present Times.* London: Basil Blackwell, 1985.

Barbach, Lonnie. *For Yourself: The Fulfillment of Female Sexuality.* Garden City, N.Y.: Doubleday Anchor, 1976.

———, ed. *Pleasures: Women Write Erotica.* New York: Harper Perennial, 1985.

———, ed. *Erotic Interludes.* New York: Harper Perennial, 1987.

Belzer, Edwin G., Jr. "A Review of Female Ejaculation and the Grafenberg Spot." *Women & Health* 9 (Spring 1984).

Bernard, Jessie. *The Future of Marriage.* New York: Bantam Books, 1973.

Berne, Eric. *Transactional Analysis.* New York: Grove Press, 1961.

Blumstein, Philip, and Pepper Schwartz. *American Couples.* New York: William Morrow, 1983.

Brown, Norman O. *Life Against Death.* New York: Vintage Books, 1959.

Bruckner, Gene. *Giovanni and Lusanna.* Berkeley: University of California Press, 1986.

Caplan, Pat, ed. *The Cultural Construction of Sexuality.* London: Tavistock Publications, 1987.

Chodorow, Nancy. *The Reproduction of Mothering.* Berkeley: University of California Press, 1978.

Costello, John. *Virtue Under Fire.* Boston: Little, Brown, 1985.

Davis, Murray S. *Smut.* Chicago: University of Chicago Press, 1983.

D'Emilio, John. *Sexual Politics, Sexual Communities.* Chicago: University of Chicago Press, 1983.

——— and Estelle B. Freedman. *Intimate Matters: A History of Sexuality in America.* New York: Harper & Row, 1988.

Dimen, Muriel. *Surviving Sexual Contradictions.* New York: Macmillan Publishing, 1986.

———. "Power, Sexuality, and Intimacy." In Susan Bordo and Alison M. Jaggar, eds. *Gender/Body/Knowledge.* New Brunswick: Rutgers University Press, 1989.

Dinnerstein, Dorothy. *The Mermaid and the Minotaur*. New York: Harper & Row, 1976.

Dodson, Betty. *Sex for One: The Joy of Selfloving*. New York: Harmony Books, 1988.

Douglas, Jack D., and Freda Cruse Atwell. *Love, Intimacy, and Sex*. Beverly Hills: Sage Publications, 1988.

Ehrenreich, Barbara. *The Hearts of Men: American Dreams and the Flight from Commitment*. Garden City, N.Y.: Anchor Press/Doubleday, 1983.

Ehrenreich, Barbara, Elizabeth Hess and Gloria Jacobs. *Remaking Love: The Feminization of Sex*. Garden City, N.Y.: Anchor Books, 1987.

Ewen, Stuart. *Captains of Consciousness*. New York: McGraw-Hill, 1977.

———— and Elizabeth Ewen. *Channels of Desire*. New York: McGraw-Hill, 1982.

Fass, Paula S. *The Damned and the Beautiful*. New York: Oxford University Press, 1977.

Feirstein, Bruce. *Nice Guys Sleep Alone*. New York: Dell, 1986.

Forrest, Jacqueline D., and Richard B. Fordyce. "U.S. Women's Contraceptive Attitudes and Practice: How Have They Changed in the 1980s?" *Family Planning Perspectives* 20, 3 (May/June 1988): 112–118.

Foucault, Michel. *The History of Sexuality*. New York: Vintage Books, 1980.

————. *The Use of Pleasure*. New York: Vintage Books, 1986.

————. *The Care of the Self*. New York: Vintage Books, 1988.

Friedan, Betty. *The Feminine Mystique*. New York: W. W. Norton, 1963.

Freud, Sigmund. *Civilization and Its Discontents*. New York: W. W. Norton, 1961.

————. *Three Essays on the Theory of Sexuality*. New York: Avon Books, 1962.

Gaylin, Willard, and Ethel Person, eds. *Passionate Attachments: Thinking About Love*. New York: Free Press, 1988.

Gilligan, Carol. *In a Different Voice: Psychological Theory and Women's Development*. Cambridge, Mass.: Harvard University Press, 1982.

Gitlin, Todd. *The Sixties: Years of Hope, Days of Rage*. New York: Bantam Books, 1987.

Glassner, Barry. *Bodies*. New York: G. P. Putnam's, 1988.

Goode, William J. "Why Men Resist." *Dissent* (Spring 1980).

Helsing, Knud J., Moyses Szklo and George W. Comstock. "Factors Associated with Mortality After Widowhood," *American Journal of Public Health* 71 (1981): 802–809.

Hite, Shere. *Women and Love: A Cultural Revolution in Progress*. New York: Alfred A. Knopf, 1987.

Hochschild, Arlie. *The Second Shift: Working Parents and the Revolution at Home*. New York: Viking Press, 1989.

Hofferth, Sandra L., Joan R. Kahn and Wendy Baldwin. "Premarital Sexual Activity Among U.S. Teenage Women over the Past Three Decades." *Family Planning Perspectives* 19 (March 1987): 46–53.

Horn, Maurice. *Sex in the Comics.* New York: Chelsea House, 1985.

Isay, Richard A. *Being Homosexual: Gay Men and Their Development.* New York: Farrar, Straus & Giroux, 1989.

Israel, Betsy. *Grown-up Fast.* New York: Poseidon Press, 1988.

Jones, Elise F., et al. *Teenage Pregnancy in Industrialized Countries.* New Haven: Yale University Press, 1986.

Kinsey, Alfred C., et al. *Sexual Behavior in the Human Female.* Philadelphia: W. B. Saunders, 1953.

Komarovsky, Mirra. *Dilemmas of Masculinity.* New York: W. W. Norton, 1976.

Lasch, Christopher. *The Culture of Narcissism.* New York: W. W. Norton, 1979.

————. *The Minimal Self.* New York: W. W. Norton, 1984.

Lawson, Annette. *Adultery.* New York: Basic Books, 1988.

Leites, Edmund. *The Puritan Conscience and Modern Sexuality.* New Haven: Yale University Press, 1986.

Luker, Kristin. *Taking Chances: Abortion and the Decision Not to Contracept.* Berkeley: University of California Press, 1975.

————. *Abortion and the Politics of Motherhood.* Berkeley: University of California Press, 1984.

Marchand, Roland. *Advertising and the American Dream.* Berkeley: University of California Press, 1985.

Marcuse, Herbert. *Eros and Civilization.* Boston: Beacon Press, 1955.

————. *One-Dimensional Man.* Boston: Beacon Press, 1964.

Maslow, Abraham. *Toward a Psychology of Being.* New York: Van Nostrand, 1962.

————. *The Farther Reaches of Human Nature.* New York: Viking Press, 1971.

May, Elaine Tyler. *Great Expectations.* Chicago: University of Chicago Press, 1980.

May, Henry R. *Coming to Terms.* Berkeley: University of California Press, 1987.

May, Rollo. *Existential Psychology.* New York: Random House, 1961.

————. *Love and Will.* New York: W. W. Norton, 1969.

McCarthy, Barry. *Male Sexual Awareness.* New York: Carroll & Graf, 1988.

Moffatt, Michael. *Coming of Age in New Jersey.* New Brunswick: Rutgers University Press, 1989.

Muscatine, Charles. *The Old French Fabliaux.* New Haven: Yale University Press, 1986.

Nelson, Peter. *Real Man Tells All.* New York: Penguin, 1988.

Perls, Frederick S. *Gestalt Therapy Verbatim.* New York: Bantam Books, 1971.

Perrett, Geoffrey. *American History in the Twenties.* New York: Touchstone Books, 1982.

Reich, Wilhelm. *Character Analysis.* New York: Farrar, Straus & Giroux, 1949.

————. *The Sexual Revolution.* New York: Noonday Press, 1962.

————. *The Function of the Orgasm.* New York: Pocket Books, 1963.

Riesman, David, et al. *The Lonely Crowd.* Garden City, N.Y.: Doubleday Anchor, 1956.

Robinson, John P. "Who's Doing the Housework?" *American Demographics* (December 1988): 24–28, 63.

Robinson, Paul. *The Modernization of Sex.* New York: Harper Colophon, 1976.

Rogers, Carl. *On Becoming a Person.* Boston: Houghton Mifflin, 1961.

Rothman, Ellen K. *Hands and Hearts.* New York: Basic Books, 1984.

Rothman, Sheila M. *Women's Proper Place.* New York: Basic Books, 1978.

Rubin, Lillian Breslow. *Worlds of Pain: Life in the Working-Class Family.* New York: Basic/Harper Torchbook, 1976.

Rubin, Lillian B. *Intimate Strangers: Men and Women Together.* New York: Harper Perennial Library, 1984.

Russell, Bertrand. *Marriage and Morals.* New York: Bantam Books, 1959.

Schur, Edwin M. *The Americanization of Sex.* Philadelphia: Temple University Press, 1988.

Shilts, Randy. *And the Band Played On: Politics, People and the AIDS Epidemic.* New York: St. Martin's Press, 1987.

Smith-Rosenberg, Carroll. *Disorderly Conduct: Visions of Gender in Victorian America.* New York: Oxford University Press, 1985.

Snitow, Ann, Christine Stansell and Sharon Thompson, eds. *Powers of Desire: The Politics of Sexuality.* New York: Monthly Review Press, 1983.

Stansell, Christine. *City of Women.* Urbana: University of Illinois Press, 1987.

Stone, Lawrence. "Passionate Attachments in the West in Historical Perspective." In William Gaylin and Ethel Persons, eds. *Passionate Attachments: Thinking About Love.* New York: Free Press, 1988.

Storr, Anthony. *Solitude.* New York: Free Press, 1988.

Stout, James W., and Frederick T. Rivara. "Schools and Sex Education: Does It Work?" *Pediatrics* 83, 3 (March 1989): 375–379.

Susser, Mervyn, "Widowhood: A Situational Life Stress or a Stressful Event?" *American Journal of Public Health* 71 (1981): 793–796.

Sutich, A. J., and M. A. Vich. *Readings in Humanistic Psychology.* New York: Free Press, 1969.

Swidler, Ann. "Love and Adulthood in American Culture." In Neil Smelser and Erik Erikson, eds. *Themes of Work and Love in Adulthood.* Cambridge, Mass.: Harvard University Press, 1980.

Tannahill, Reay. *Sex in History.* New York: Scarborough Books, 1982.

Thompson, Sharon. "Search for Tomorrow: On Feminism and the Reconstruction of Teen Romance." In Carole S. Vance, ed. *Pleasure and Danger: Exploring Female Sexuality.* Boston: Routledge & Kegan Paul, 1984.

Tiefer, Leonore. "In Pursuit of the Perfect Penis." *American Behavioral Scientist* 29, 5 (May–June 1986): 579–599.

———. "Social Constructionism and the Study of Human Sexuality." In P. Shaver and C. Hendrick, eds. *Sex & Gender.* Newbury Park, Calif.: Sage Publications, 1987.

Valverde, Mariana. "Beyond Gender Dangers and Private Pleasures: Theory and Ethics in the Sex Debate." *Feminist Studies* 15, 2 (Summer 1989): 237–254.

Vance, Carole S., ed. *Pleasure and Danger: Exploring Female Sexuality.* Boston: Routledge & Kegan Paul, 1984.

Weeks, Jeffrey. *Sexuality and Its Discontents.* London: Routledge & Kegan Paul, 1985.